Work and Families

Lynda Macdonald

. Croner
a Wolters Kluwer business

Wolters Kluwer (UK) Limited
145 London Road
Kingston upon Thames
Surrey KT2 6SR
Tel: 020 8247 1175

Published by
Wolters Kluwer (UK) Limited
145 London Road
Kingston upon Thames
Surrey KT2 6SR
Tel: 020 8247 1175

First published April 2002
Second Edition 2005
Third Edition 2007
Fourth Edition 2015
© Wolters Kluwer (UK) Limited

Crown copyright material is reproduced under the terms of the
Open Government Licence.
Although great care has been taken in the compilation and preparation of this work to
ensure accuracy, the publishers cannot in any circumstances accept responsibility for
any errors or omissions.

Subscribers to this book should be aware that only Acts of Parliament and Statutory
Instruments have the force of law and that only the courts can authoritatively interpret
the law.

ISBN 978–1–85524–785–7

Printed by Gutenberg Press Ltd, Malta

Contents

CHAPTER 1

MATERNITY RIGHTS

INTRODUCTION

All pregnant employees (whether part time, full time, permanent or temporary) have the statutory right, subject to certain notification requirements, to take up to 52 weeks' maternity leave and resume working afterwards. The maternity leave period is made up of 26 weeks' ordinary maternity leave and a further 26 weeks' additional maternity leave which begins on the day after the ordinary maternity leave period ends.

Most employees who take maternity leave will be eligible to receive statutory maternity pay (SMP) for up to 39 weeks during their absence on maternity leave. Employers may recover most of the SMP they have paid out from the Government.

The right to maternity leave and the right to receive SMP are contained in separate pieces of legislation and are based on separate criteria. To an extent, they operate independently of one another.

Under provisions introduced by the **Shared Parental Leave Regulations 2014**, employees whose child was born on or after 5 April 2015 and who have the right to maternity leave have the choice to end their maternity leave on a date they specify and switch to "shared parental leave". This enables them to share the untaken balance of their leave (and pay) with their husband, partner, civil partner or the father of the child, subject to certain rules and requirements. Shared parental leave is explored fully in chapter four.

MATERNITY LEAVE

Entitlement

All employees who become pregnant have the right to take 52 consecutive weeks' maternity leave, regardless of their length of service, age or marital status. Maternity leave is available only to employees, ie those engaged on contracts of employment, and not to other workers such as contractors, agency staff, casual workers or self-employed people. Entitlement extends equally to both permanent and temporary employees and to part-time employees as well as full-time employees.

Maternity rights are unaffected if more than one child is born as a result of the same pregnancy (for example, twins or triplets).

Surrogacy Arrangements

A woman who acts as a surrogate mother is entitled to statutory maternity leave and pay in the same way as any other mother.

The European Court of Justice (ECJ) has held (in *CD v ST* [2013] ECJ Case C-167/12) that commissioning mothers under a surrogacy arrangement do not have the right to maternity leave under the EU Pregnant Workers Directive. The ECJ stated that the purpose of maternity leave under the Pregnant Workers Directive is "to protect the health of the mother ... arising from her pregnancy". Consequently, a woman who has received a baby through a surrogacy arrangement is not entitled to maternity leave as she will not have been pregnant.

As from 5 April 2015, however, commissioning parents in a surrogacy arrangement have the right to adoption leave provided they have applied, or intend to apply, for a parental order. Under a parental order, a child born to a surrogate mother is treated in law as the commissioning parents' own child. An employee taking adoption leave may also qualify for statutory adoption pay, subject to his or her meeting the normal eligibility conditions. However, only one of the parents can take adoption leave while the other parent may be able to take paternity leave (provided he or she meets the relevant eligibility conditions). Adoption leave and pay are fully explored in chapter three.

Timing of Maternity Leave

Maternity leave is made up of 26 weeks' ordinary maternity leave followed immediately by a further 26 weeks' additional maternity leave. Additional maternity leave starts on the day after the ordinary maternity leave period ends. Maternity leave must be taken in one block; it is not permitted to take a period of maternity leave, then return to work, then take another period of maternity leave.

An employee who is pregnant has the right to choose when she begins her period of maternity leave which can be any time on or after the beginning of the 11th week before her expected week of childbirth (EWC). There are two exceptions, which are:

- where the employee gives birth prematurely
- where the employee is absent from work due to a pregnancy-related condition or illness within four weeks of the date the baby is due.

Unless one of these exceptions applies, the employee may delay the start of her maternity leave until a time of her own choosing and may, for example, continue to work right up until the day the baby is born. Maternity leave cannot begin, however, before the start of the 11th week before the EWC.

Employees also have the choice to take their full entitlement of 52 weeks' maternity leave or to return to work at any time between the end of the two-week period following the birth (or four-week period for manual workers) and the expiry of the 52 weeks (subject to notice requirements).

Premature births

If an employee who has not yet started her maternity leave gives birth prematurely, her maternity leave will begin on the day after the date of childbirth. In these circumstances, the employee must notify her employer of the birth as soon as is reasonably practicable. If she has not already done so, she must also inform her employer of the EWC and provide a Form Mat B1 (certificate of expected confinement) accompanied by Form Mat B2 (certificate of confinement) or an equivalent document, signed by her doctor or midwife, confirming the date on which the birth occurred. Form Mat B2 is to be found on the reverse side of Form Mat B1.

Childbirth is defined to include the birth of a living child (however premature), or of a child living or dead after 24 weeks of pregnancy. Employees who give birth after 24 weeks of pregnancy are, therefore, entitled to maternity leave and SMP (subject to the standard qualifying conditions) in the normal way, even in the event of a stillbirth.

If an employee loses her baby before reaching the 25th week of her pregnancy, she will not be entitled to maternity leave or SMP. Her absence from work should be treated as sickness absence and she may be entitled to statutory sick pay and/or contractual sick pay until such time as she recovers and is in a position to return to work.

3

Absence due to pregnancy-related condition or illness

If an employee is absent from work with a pregnancy-related illness or condition on or after the beginning of the fourth week before her EWC, her maternity leave period is triggered automatically. In these circumstances, maternity leave begins either on the first day of the fourth week before the EWC or on the day immediately following the day on which she was taken ill, whichever occurs sooner. This is irrespective of whether that day falls before the date the employee previously notified as the date on which she intended to start her maternity leave. In these circumstances, the employee must inform her employer as soon as is reasonably practicable that she is absent from work wholly or partly because of pregnancy.

Employers may, if they choose to do so, disregard odd days of pregnancy-related sickness absence within four weeks of the EWC, but may need to be reassured by the employee's GP or an occupational doctor that the employee is fit to remain at work.

Compulsory Maternity Leave

The period of two weeks starting with the date of childbirth is known as "compulsory maternity leave". Under s.72 of the **Employment Rights Act 1996**, an employer must not permit an employee to do any work during the compulsory maternity leave period. If the employee does manual work, for example, in a factory, then no return to work is permitted within four weeks of the birth (under the **Public Health Act 1936**).

An employer that permits an employee to return to work before the end of the compulsory maternity leave period is guilty of an offence and liable, on summary conviction, to a fine of up to £500.

Notification Requirements

To exercise her right to maternity leave, a pregnant employee must comply with certain notification requirements. She must inform her employer (in writing if requested by the employer) by the end of the 15th week before the EWC (which is known as the "qualifying week"):

- that she is pregnant
- of her EWC
- of the date on which she intends her maternity leave to start.

If it is not reasonably practicable for the employee to provide this notification to her employer by the end of the qualifying week, she must do so as soon as it is reasonably practicable.

This notification of the date on which the employee intends to start her maternity leave covers both ordinary maternity leave and additional maternity leave. There is no need for the employee to give notice that she intends to start additional maternity leave at the end of her ordinary maternity leave unless she has previously stated that she intended to return to work at the end of ordinary maternity leave. In this case, she would need to give her employer eight weeks' notice of her revised return-to-work date (see below).

The employer has the right to require the employee to state her intentions regarding the date on which she intends her maternity leave to start in writing and to produce a Form Mat B1 (certificate of expected confinement), or an equivalent document, signed by her doctor or registered midwife. The employer should retain either the original or a copy of the certificate on file if the employee is entitled to SMP.

Change of mind
An employee who has notified her employer of the date on which she wishes her maternity leave to begin may change her mind about the start date, so long as she informs the employer of that fact and gives at least 28 days' notice of the revised start date or the original start date, whichever falls first.

Employer's response to notification
Once an employee has provided proper notification of her intention to take maternity leave, the employer must respond in writing within 28 days to tell her when she is due to return. Where the employee has changed her mind about when to start her maternity leave, the deadline for writing to tell her when she is due to return is 28 days from the start of her leave period.

Specifically, the employer must write to the employee acknowledging her intentions and informing her of the latest date on which she must return to work after her maternity leave. This date will fall 52 weeks after the date the employee's maternity leave is due to begin. From this, the employee will be clear as to when she is expected to return to work if she takes her full 52-week entitlement of maternity leave.

It is safe for the employer to assume that this is the date of return unless the employee has stated that she does not intend to take her full entitlement and has given an earlier return to work date. In these circumstances, the employee will still be entitled to change her mind regarding her return date simply by notifying her employer at least eight weeks' in advance of the originally notified return date that she wishes to take the full 52 weeks' entitlement. Alternatively, if she later decides to return earlier than the previously notified date, she must give eight weeks' notice of the earlier return date (see below).

If the employer fails to respond to the employee's notification within 28 days and/or does not tell the employee when she is due to return to work, it will not be possible to prevent her from returning to work early without giving the proper notice, nor will it be possible to discipline or dismiss her for failing to return to work on time.

SUSPENSION FROM WORK DURING PREGNANCY

Sections 66–70 of the **Employment Rights Act 1996** set down certain health and safety provisions for the protection of pregnant women at work. The key principle underlying these provisions is that, if a pregnant employee's work could in any way place her or her unborn child at risk, the employer is under a duty to take steps to remove her from that risk. A failure to take the necessary steps to protect a pregnant employee's health and safety (or that of her unborn child) will be a breach of the general statutory duty to take care of the health, safety and welfare of employees at work under the **Health and Safety at Work, etc Act 1974**.

The practical effect of these provisions is that employers are under a duty to ensure that pregnant employees are not required to perform any work that could put their health or safety, or that of their unborn child, at risk. The risk could arise from the employee's job duties, her working conditions, work processes or the working environment.

It should be noted that the provisions in place to protect the health and safety of pregnant employees apply where an employee is able to come to work (ie she is in good health), but is unable to perform her full range of job duties for health or safety reasons. The provisions do not arise in consequence of an employee being ill and signed off sick by her doctor.

Where a risk to a pregnant employee's health or safety is identified (often as a result of a risk assessment), the employer must do one of the following:

• alter the employee's job duties or working conditions so as to remove the risk or reduce it to an acceptable level

- transfer the employee temporarily to suitable alternative work
- suspend the employee on full pay until the start of her maternity leave.

The above requirements stand to be applied in the order given, ie the employer should first seek to alter the employee's job duties or working conditions before considering a transfer to a different job; and should only suspend the employee if no suitable alternative work is available or if the available alternative work would not remove or sufficiently reduce the risks to the employee's health or safety.

Suitable Alternative Work

Section 67(2) of the **Employment Rights Act 1996** stipulates that for alternative work to be suitable, it must be:
- appropriate for the employee to do in the circumstances, and
- on terms and conditions that are not substantially less favourable to the employee than those of her normal job.

Where it is not possible for the employer to offer alternative work to a pregnant employee whose work places her health or safety at risk, then the employer must suspend the employee from work until the start of her maternity leave (or until it is safe for her to resume working if that occurs sooner). This course of action is a last resort and should not be imposed if suitable alternative work is available.

If the employee unreasonably refuses an offer of suitable alternative work, she may be suspended from work without pay. Before taking such drastic action, however, the employer would need to be sure that the alternative work that was offered was suitable for the employee to do, that it was on terms no less favourable to the employee than those of her normal job, and that the employee's refusal to undertake the work was, in fact, unreasonable.

Employees who Work at Night

Where an employee who works at nights becomes pregnant, the employer must, if recommended by her doctor, move her to day-shift working. This is because there is an obligation under the **Management of Health and Safety at Work Regulations 1992** not to oblige employees who are pregnant to work night shifts. Similar protection is afforded to women for a period following childbirth.

The employer must also suspend a new or expectant mother who works at nights if a certificate from a registered medical practitioner or midwife identifies a period during which she should not work.

Pay During Suspension

Suspension from work in these circumstances must be on full pay. In *Gassmayr v Bundesministerin für Wissenschaft und Forschung* [2010] ECJ Case C-194/08, however, the ECJ held that a pregnant employee who was suspended from work due to a health risk was not entitled to continue to be paid an emergency on-call allowance while suspended, as she was not available to be called out. The ECJ ruled that it was permissible for an employer to withhold allowances that depend on performing a specific task (but not those which do not depend on performance).

In the earlier case of *British Airways (European Operations at Gatwick) v (1) Moore (2) Botterill* [2000] IRLR 296, the Employment Appeal Tribunal (EAT) held that transferring pregnant cabin crew to ground duties did not amount to suitable alternative employment because the alternative jobs, although offered on the same basic pay, excluded the flying allowances that were paid as part of the employee's normal remuneration package. Part of the flying allowance was paid to cover out-of-pocket expenses and part represented profit in the hands of the employees. The EAT held that, while the employees were prevented from undertaking flying duties because of pregnancy, they were entitled to retain the part of their flying allowances which represented profit.

RIGHTS DURING MATERNITY LEAVE

Status of Contract of Employment

An employee has the right to the continuation of all her contractual terms and conditions of employment, except pay, throughout both ordinary and additional maternity leave. Terms may include, for example, use of a company car, use of company mobile phone or laptop, health insurance cover and accrual of holiday entitlement (see below) that would have applied to the employee but for her absence.

There is no duty on employers to continue an employee's normal wage or salary during maternity leave (although statutory maternity pay may be payable — see below).

Following the case of *Hoyland v Asda Stores Ltd* [2006] IRLR 468, it appears that if an annual attendance bonus is part of the employee's contractual entitlement (as opposed to a purely discretionary benefit), such a bonus may be reduced *pro rata* to reflect the employee's period of absence on ordinary or additional maternity leave. This is because a contractual bonus constitutes part of remuneration, which need not be continued during maternity leave. In contrast, if a bonus is discretionary, or is one that does not relate to attendance or to the amount of work done, it is likely to be unlawful to withhold any part of it from the employee on account of absence on maternity leave.

Following the implementation of the **Maternity and Parental Leave, etc and the Paternity and Adoption Leave (Amendment) Regulations 2008**, however, an employee on maternity leave is entitled to be granted any discretionary bonus in respect of the two-week compulsory maternity leave period (see above). This two-week period must, therefore, be taken into account when calculating discretionary bonus entitlement for an employee on maternity leave, irrespective of the status or purpose of the bonus.

Accrual of Holiday Entitlement

Under the EU Working Time Directive (2003/88/EC), all workers must be granted at least four weeks' paid statutory annual leave. Under the UK's **Working Time Regulations 1998**, this period of annual leave was extended to 5.6 weeks (which can include any paid public holidays). Many employers go further and grant their employees contractual holiday leave in excess of the statutory 5.6 weeks per annum.

Employees who are on maternity leave are entitled to continue to accrue both statutory and contractual annual leave throughout their periods of maternity leave. Where, due to absence on maternity leave, the employee has been unable to take all her statutory annual leave, she must be permitted to carry it forward to the next holiday year and take it during that year.

If there has been a workplace shutdown for the purpose of annual holidays, an employee who is on maternity leave at that time will be entitled to take an equivalent period of statutory annual leave at another time. A decision by the European Court of Justice (in *Merino Gómez v Continental Industrias del Caucho* SA ECJ Case C-342/01) made it clear that statutory annual leave and maternity leave are for entirely different purposes and an employee is, therefore, entitled to take annual leave at a time other than during her maternity leave.

By extension, the same principle would apply to employees who are on paternity leave, adoption leave or shared parental leave at the time of an annual holiday shutdown.

Pension Contributions

Special provisions apply to pension contributions during maternity leave. The **Social Security Act 1989** (paragraph 5, schedule 5) specifies that during ordinary maternity leave and during any period of additional maternity leave which is paid (pay in this context includes SMP), an employee is entitled to continue to accrue benefits under any occupational pension scheme as if she was working normally. Pension benefits must also continue for a minimum of 39 weeks for employees on maternity leave who, due to short service, are not eligible for SMP.

If an employee contributes to the pension scheme, her contributions can be reduced, where appropriate, in line with the pay she is receiving from the employer. The employer must, however, continue to contribute to the scheme based on the employee's normal rate of pay.

Keeping-in-touch Days

A provision introduced by the **Work and Families Act 2006** allows for "keeping-in-touch days" (KIT days) during an employee's maternity leave. This allows an employee on maternity leave to go into work for up to 10 days (which may be either single days or combined in one or more blocks) without triggering the end of her maternity leave or losing any statutory maternity pay. This provision does not, however, allow the period of maternity leave to be extended beyond a total of 52 weeks.

KIT days can only be worked by agreement, ie the employer cannot insist that an employee on maternity leave must come in to work, nor does the employee have any right to be offered any work. Where an employee works for part of a day, this counts as a full day for this purpose.

KIT days can, by agreement, be arranged for any type of work but will often be used to allow an employee to attend a training course, be present at an important meeting or simply to allow her to keep up to date with a particular job or project.

Where KIT days are arranged, the employer must agree with the employee the rate of payment for the days worked. The employee will be entitled to be paid under the terms of her contract of employment. Any statutory or contractual maternity pay may be offset against the employee's wages/salary for the days in question.

Reasonable Contact

Employers are entitled to maintain reasonable contact with employees who are on maternity leave. This may, for example, be in order to discuss the employee's plans for returning to work or to provide her with an update on developments in the workplace. This provision is in addition to the KIT days provision.

Employees also have the right to make reasonable contact with their employers while on maternity leave.

RIGHTS IF JOB IS REDUNDANT DURING MATERNITY LEAVE

Consultation

As a result of the implementation of the **Maternity and Parental Leave, etc and the Paternity and Adoption Leave (Amendment) Regulations 2008** (SI 2008 No. 1966), an employee on maternity leave is entitled to be consulted if her employer is contemplating making her job redundant or is proposing any change to her job role.

Any failure to carry out such consultation is likely to amount to unlawful sex discrimination.

Additionally, selections for redundancy must be carried out fairly and must not discriminate against women who are on maternity leave at the time.

Selection for Redundancy

In the Latvian case of *Riezniece v Zemkopibas Ministrija* [2013] ECJ Case No. C-7/12, the employee was selected for redundancy while she was absent from work on "parental leave" (the principles of this decision apply to UK employees on maternity leave). The employer had used performance criteria to make the redundancy selections, and employees who were working normally were assessed on the basis of their most recent appraisals. The employee was assessed on the basis of her last appraisal which had taken place before she began her period of leave (some 18 months earlier). However, because different methods of appraisal had been in place at that time, she was assessed using different criteria which were less favourable to her.

The employee brought claims to the Latvian court arguing that her treatment was discriminatory. The case was referred through to the ECJ. She also complained that, although she had been offered and had accepted an alternative post, this post was abolished three months later and the employer had been aware that this would happen at the time she had been offered it. Consequently, she argued, she had been denied the opportunity to return to work in an equivalent role.

The ECJ ruled that, where a much higher number of women than men take parental leave, employers must not use different redundancy selection criteria to assess employees on parental leave compared to the criteria applied to employees who are working normally. Although it is permissible for an employer to assess an employee who is absent from work on the basis of her most recent period of actual work, it is not permitted to use different criteria for such assessments. Identical selection criteria must be applied to all employees when determining whom to select for redundancy.

The ECJ also held that it is impermissible for an employer to offer an employee who has the right to return to work a post which it knows is set to be abolished.

Right to be Offered a Suitable Available Vacancy

Where an employee is made redundant during either ordinary or additional maternity leave, she has the right (before the termination of her employment under her existing contract) to be offered any suitable available vacancy that exists either with her employer or an associate or successor employer. This is the case irrespective of the fact that the employee may not be in a position to take up the new job straight away (ie she may have several months of maternity leave still outstanding). The offer must be made before the ending of employment under the existing contract and the new contract must take effect immediately on the ending of that contract. A "suitable available vacancy" is an alternative job which is:

- suitable and appropriate for the employee to do in the circumstances, and
- on terms that are not substantially less favourable to her than those of her previous contract, including provisions concerning capacity and place of work.

Legislation requires that an employee on maternity leave must be given priority over any other redundant employees who are not on maternity leave (or additional paternity leave, adoption leave or shared parental leave) in respect of available suitable positions. This is the case even if the employee on maternity leave is not the best candidate for a particular vacant position — provided she meets the essential criteria for the post.

This principle was aptly demonstrated in the case of *Sefton Borough Council v Wainwright* EAT 0168/14. The employer had decided (as part of a cost-saving restructuring exercise) to merge two equally graded posts, one occupied by Ms Wainwright and the other by Mr Pierce. Shortly, after Ms Wainwright had begun a period of maternity leave, both she and Mr Pierce were notified that they were at risk of redundancy and both were interviewed for the new post. It was accepted that both were qualified for the role, but the employer thought that Mr Pierce was the better candidate and so appointed him to the post. Having been made redundant, Ms Wainwright complained to an employment tribunal that her redundancy dismissal was automatically unfair and discriminatory on account of the employer's failure to offer her an available suitable post.

It was accepted that the newly created post was "suitable" for Ms Wainwright and so the EAT ruled that the employer should have appointed her to it without requiring her to compete, notwithstanding that management believed Mr Pierce to be the better candidate. The duty to offer the post to Ms Wainwright arose as soon as the employer had made the decision to merge the two roles. Consequently, Ms Wainwright's dismissal was automatically unfair. The EAT found, however, that the employer's actions did not amount to discrimination on grounds of pregnancy or maternity leave. Even though the employer's failure to offer Ms Wainwright the vacant post coincided with her being on maternity leave, it did not automatically follow that the failure to appoint her to the post was because she was on maternity leave.

If there is no suitable work available for an employee on maternity leave whose job is redundant, the employer may lawfully terminate her contract on grounds of redundancy. In this case, the employee will be entitled to a statutory redundancy payment provided she has at least two years' continuous service, and possibly (depending on the terms of her contract of employment) a contractual payment as well. She will also be entitled to pay in lieu of notice in accordance with her contract.

Additionally, if an employee on maternity leave unreasonably refuses to accept an offer of suitable alternative employment, the employer may make her redundant, although in these circumstances the employee may lose her right to statutory redundancy pay.

Essentially, a failure to offer alternative employment to an employee on maternity leave whose job is redundant may be justified before an employment tribunal on either of the above grounds (provided the employer has the necessary evidence to present to the tribunal).

PREGNANCY/MATERNITY DISCRIMINATION

Special protection against discriminatory treatment is available to women who become pregnant and take maternity leave. The **Equality Act 2010**, s.18, provides that any unfavourable treatment of an employee will be unlawful if it is because of pregnancy, illness suffered as a result of pregnancy or because she has indicated an intention to take, is taking, or has taken maternity leave. There is no defence to this type of discrimination, no matter how much inconvenience may be caused to the employer as a result of an employee's pregnancy or absence on maternity leave.

An employee who is pregnant and who is treated unfavourably for a pregnancy-related reason does not need to compare her treatment with that of any other employee (whether male or female) in order to found a discrimination claim at an employment tribunal. The same principle applies to employees on maternity leave. There is no minimum period of qualifying service required to bring a claim of pregnancy/maternity discrimination to an employment tribunal and, where a claim is upheld, unlimited compensation may be awarded, including compensation for injury to feelings.

Examples of discriminatory treatment could include:

- denying an employee promotion because she is pregnant or absent on maternity leave
- excluding an employee from training on account of her pregnancy or absence on maternity leave
- moving a pregnant employee to another job so that she no longer comes into contact with customers or clients
- disciplining a pregnant employee on account of time off work for pregnancy-related sickness.

In *Nixon v Ross Coates Solicitors and anor* EAT 0108/10, a pregnant employee succeeded in her complaints of sex and pregnancy harassment due to the upset and embarrassment she experienced when the HR manager at the firm where she worked began gossiping with other employees about who the father of her baby was.

The dismissal of an employee because of pregnancy or maternity leave will also amount to an automatically unfair dismissal under the **Employment Rights Act 1996**, and no minimum period of continuous service is required to bring such a claim to tribunal.

The "Protected Period"

The special protection against discriminatory treatment described above is available to women throughout what is known as the "protected period", which is the period commencing with the beginning of pregnancy and terminating at the end of maternity leave or when the employee returns to work, if earlier. Additionally, if the discriminatory treatment complained of occurs after the protected period, but is nevertheless the result of a decision taken during that period, then it will be regarded as having occurred during the protected period.

In *Lyons v DWP JobCentre Plus* [2014] EAT 0348/13, however, the EAT held that the dismissal of an employee for absences due to post-natal depression which occurred after the end of her maternity leave did not amount to pregnancy or maternity discrimination. This was because — although the employee's illness was pregnancy-related — the unfavourable treatment about which she complained (ie the decision to dismiss her) occurred outside the protected period. Nor could her complaint of sex discrimination succeed because an employer is entitled to take sickness absence which occurs after the end of the protected period into account in the normal way when reviewing whether an employee's level of absence justifies dismissal.

This "protected period" provision does not, however, permit employers to afford women who are pregnant or on maternity leave any type of favourable treatment. The EAT, in *Eversheds Legal Services Ltd v De Belin* [2011] IRLR 448, ruled that the obligation to protect employees who are pregnant or on maternity leave relates only to what is "reasonably necessary to compensate them for the disadvantages occasioned by their condition". The more favourable treatment must represent proportionate action to compensate them for the disadvantages caused by pregnancy or maternity leave.

There is a specific provision in the **Equality Act 2010** to the effect that special treatment of women in connection with pregnancy or childbirth does not amount to unlawful discrimination against men. Male employees who claim that affording female employees maternity benefits amounts to discrimination against them on grounds of their sex cannot, therefore, bring successful claims of sex discrimination.

Women who have IVF Treatment

A woman undergoing in vitro fertilisation (IVF) treatment is regarded as pregnant, and so protected against discriminatory treatment on pregnancy grounds, only once in vitro fertilised eggs are transferred into her uterus. Additionally, however, a woman is protected against sex discrimination (not pregnancy discrimination) during the very short period following the laboratory fertilisation of the eggs and before the implantation into her uterus — usually four to six days. Employers should, therefore, be alert to the special protection afforded to women undergoing that particular stage of IVF treatment after the eggs have been fertilised but before implantation into the uterus. Following implantation, the woman is regarded as being pregnant.

If the IVF treatment is successful and the woman remains pregnant she will be protected against discriminatory treatment until she returns to work after maternity leave.

If the treatment is unsuccessful, the woman's special protection ends four weeks after the date of implantation. A pregnancy test is normally taken two weeks after the implantation of an embryo, and so the woman will have special protection for those two weeks and, if the pregnancy test is negative, for a further two weeks thereafter.

Surrogate Mothers

The commissioning mother in a surrogacy arrangement does not have the right to maternity leave simply because she will not have been pregnant. This was confirmed by the European Court of Justice in *CD v ST* [2013] ECJ Case C-167/12 in which the ECJ was tasked with judging whether a woman who had commissioned a surrogate mother to have a child on her behalf could claim pregnancy/maternity discrimination or sex discrimination on account of being refused maternity leave and pay by her employer. The employee claimed that her treatment was in breach of the relevant maternity provisions in the **Employment Rights Act 1996**, the **Maternity and Parental Leave, etc Regulations 1999** and the **Equality Act 2010**.

The ECJ held that, even though the commissioning mother had breastfed the baby, she had at no time been pregnant herself and, therefore, there could be no entitlement to maternity leave or pay under Article 8 of the EU Pregnant Workers Directive. Similarly, there could be no pregnancy discrimination as the employee had never been pregnant.

The ECJ also held that the employer's refusal to grant maternity leave and pay did not amount to sex discrimination as the employee had not been treated less favourably than a man who had commissioned a surrogate to have a child would have been treated. Thus, there was no breach of the EU Equal Treatment Directive.

As from 5 April 2015, however, revised legislation gives parents who commission a surrogate to have a child on their behalf (and who apply for a parental order) the right to adoption leave and statutory adoption pay (the latter being subject to the employee meeting certain eligibility conditions). Adoption leave is covered fully in chapter three.

RIGHT TO RETURN TO WORK

Where an employee chooses to return to work at the end of additional maternity leave, there is no duty on her to give any notice to her employer — she may simply turn up for work on the appointed day. The employer may, however, use the "reasonable contact" provision (see above) to discuss this matter with the employee.

If, the employee is ill and so unable to return to work on the date she is due to return, she should notify her employer of that fact in accordance with her employer's rules in relation to the notification of sickness absence. She will then be entitled to be paid statutory and/or contractual sick pay in the normal way.

If an employee who was entitled to maternity leave is not permitted to return to work at the end of the maternity leave period, or on a properly notified earlier date, she will in effect have been dismissed by the employer. Such a dismissal will be automatically unfair and the employee can bring a claim to tribunal irrespective of her length of service at the time.

Notice Requirement for an Early Return

An employee who wishes to return to work before the end of additional maternity leave, or before a previously notified return date, must notify her employer of the proposed early return date at least eight weeks before the date in question. If she does not do so, her employer may delay her return until eight weeks have elapsed or until the date on which she would otherwise have been due to return, whichever occurs sooner. In these circumstances, the employer is under no obligation to pay the employee until the full eight-week notice period has expired and she has returned to work. The employer may not, however, postpone the employee's return beyond the date that her maternity leave would have otherwise expired.

An employee is also required to give eight weeks' notice if she decides to return to work later than a previously notified return date.

There is no limit on the number of times that an employee can change her mind as to her return date provided she gives the required eight weeks' notice and provided the return date falls before the end of the period of 52 weeks' maternity leave to which all employees are entitled.

Rights on Return

Different rules are in place with regards to an employee's right to return to work depending on whether she chooses to return at or before the end of her ordinary maternity leave period (ie having taken maternity leave of 26 weeks or less) or during or at the end of additional maternity leave (ie having taken maternity leave of between 26 and 52 weeks).

An employee returning to work before or at the end of ordinary maternity leave has the right to do so in exactly the same job that she occupied before her maternity leave began.

The EAT interpreted the concept of "same job" in a wide sense in *Blundell v Governing Body of St Andrew's Catholic Primary School* [2007] IRLR 652, a case in which a primary school teacher wanted to resume work in exactly the same job as she had occupied before the start of her maternity leave, ie teaching the same class. The EAT identified three key criteria as determinative, which were:

- the nature of the work
- its capacity
- the place of work.

The EAT decided that the "nature of the work", in order to fit the requirement of the "same job", should take into account any variations to the role that were written into the employee's contract, which in this case included the school's policy of moving teachers to different classes every two years. Ms Blundell's "capacity", the EAT judged, was that of a teacher, and not as a teacher of a specific class. Finally, the "place" in which she was employed was the school, and not the particular classroom. Ms Blundell's claim, therefore, failed.

An employee who takes additional maternity leave is entitled to return to work either in the job in which she was employed before her maternity leave began or, if that is not reasonably practicable from the employer's perspective, to another job that is both suitable and appropriate for her to do in the circumstances. Any alternative job must be on terms and conditions no less favourable to the employee than those that would have applied to her but for her absence on maternity leave. Accordingly, any general pay rise that has been implemented during the employee's maternity leave must be granted to her on her return to work.

Where the employee returns to work having taken up to four weeks' parental leave immediately after her ordinary maternity leave period, her right to return to work in her original job prevails. If, however, she takes more than four weeks' parental leave immediately following on from ordinary maternity leave and if, at the end of that period, it is not reasonably practicable for her employer to permit her to return to her original job, the employer may offer her suitable alternative employment on terms and conditions no less favourable to her than those of her original job.

Where an employee takes a period of parental leave (of any length) immediately after a period of additional maternity leave, the employer may reinstate her either in her original job or, if that is not reasonably practicable, in a similar job on terms and conditions no less favourable than those to which she was entitled in her original job.

Requests for Part-time Working

It is quite common for an employee who is returning to work following maternity leave to seek to reduce her hours of work. Employers should always consider any request for a move from full-time to part-time working carefully and objectively. This is because a refusal to agree to an employee's request to move from full-time to part-time working following maternity leave may amount to indirect sex discrimination, unless the employer can objectively justify the need for the particular job to be done full time by one person (as opposed to a job-share arrangement).

Indirect sex discrimination

Indirect sex discrimination occurs where an employer applies a "provision, criterion or practice" to all employees (men and women alike), but the particular provision puts women (or men) at a disadvantage. A woman seeking to complain of indirect discrimination must also show that she was (or would have been) personally disadvantaged by the provision, criterion or practice in question.

Courts and tribunals have, over the years, frequently held that requiring a female employee with children to work full-time (as opposed to part-time) hours can amount to a provision that is indirectly discriminatory. This is because (the courts have accepted) more women than men have the primary responsibility for childcare and are consequently more likely than men to have difficulty with full-time working.

Whether it is lawful for an employer to refuse a request to move to part-time working from a woman returning to work following maternity leave will depend on whether the requirement for her to work full time can be objectively justified. Objective justification will depend on whether the employer can show that the requirement for the particular employee to work full-time hours is "proportionate to the achievement of a legitimate aim". Demonstrating that the employer had a legitimate aim will, in many cases, not be difficult, ie the aim may be to guarantee adequate manning levels or may be based on the need to meet customer demands. There is no prescribed list of "legitimate aims" and so it will be up to the employer, if challenged, to provide a sound business-based or job-based reason for any indirectly discriminatory requirement.

In addition to establishing a legitimate aim, an employer who seeks to justify the requirement for a female employee to work full time must also show that the requirement is proportionate to the achievement of the stated aim. "Proportionate" in this context means appropriate, necessary and not excessive in relation to the aim. Showing that it is proportionate to require a particular employee to work full time hours can sometimes be difficult. Essentially, the employer must demonstrate that, when viewed objectively, it was necessary (in order to achieve the aim in question) for the particular employee to work the required hours. If, for example, adequate manning levels or customer service could be maintained without requiring the employee in question to work full time, then an insistence on full-time working would not be justified.

The outcome of a particular claim for indirect sex discrimination can depend on a range of factors, including:

- the employer's overall size and administrative resources
- the number of staff employed to do the type of work in question
- the nature of the job, including whether or not the work is specialised
- the need for continuity in the work and the potential effect of part-time working on that continuity
- existing systems of organisation within the department where the employee works and the degree of cover available during periods of absence
- the level of genuine inconvenience to the business or to customers that would be caused to the employer through agreeing to a part-time working arrangement

- the extent to which the employer has made a genuine effort to accommodate the employee's request for part-time work (eg advertising for a job sharer).

Factors that are unlikely to provide objective justification for a refusal to permit part-time working include:

- opposition in principle to part-time working
- administrative inconvenience
- disruption to working arrangements to the extent that part-time working represents a deviation from previous working practices
- objections based purely on organisational policy
- opposition on the grounds that part-time working would create a precedent.

In *British Airways plc v Starmer* [2005] IRLR 862, for example, Ms Starmer, an airline pilot, asked to reduce her hours to 50% of full-time hours in order to accommodate her childcare arrangements on her return to work from maternity leave. British Airways refused the request in light of its policy requiring pilots to complete a minimum of 2000 flying hours before they could reduce their working hours to below 75% of full time. Ms Starmer lodged a claim for unlawful indirect sex discrimination on account of the rejection of her request.

The tribunal held that the relevant "provision, criterion or practice" was the requirement for Ms Starmer to work a minimum of 75% of full-time hours. It went on to conclude that this provision was to the detriment of more women than men, and was to Ms Starmer's detriment personally. The key remaining question was whether British Airways' reasons for refusing to permit a reduction to 50% hours were objectively justified. The reasons given were:

- additional training costs in relation to replacement pilots
- inability to reorganise the work among other staff
- a company ban on recruiting additional staff
- a detrimental effect on customer service and on performance
- the risk of safety being compromised.

While accepting that these aims were legitimate (with the exception of the alleged detrimental impact on customer service and performance, of which the tribunal was not convinced), the tribunal ruled that they did not outweigh the discriminatory impact on Ms Starmer. In relation to the safety argument, the tribunal held that the employer had not produced any evidence to back up its claim that safety would be compromised if the claimant was permitted to fly at 50% of full-time hours.

The tribunal, therefore, upheld Ms Starmer's claim for indirect sex discrimination and this decision was endorsed on appeal to the EAT. The EAT did, however, point out that the decision had no bearing on the general validity or lawfulness of the 2000-hour threshold. Instead, it was a decision based on the facts of the specific case.

Continuity of Employment

Since an employee's contract of employment continues throughout maternity leave for all purposes except pay, her continuity of service is preserved for statutory purposes. In other words, the period of absence must be counted when calculating the employee's total length of service for statutory purposes, such as the right to statutory redundancy pay.

Additionally, an employee returning from maternity leave must be permitted to return with her seniority, pension and other contractual rights as they would have been had she not been absent, irrespective of whether she took only ordinary maternity leave or additional maternity leave as well. In other words, the whole of the maternity leave period must be counted when calculating the employee's entitlement to service-related benefits, for example, the length of service required for a pay increase or for additional annual holiday entitlement. Similarly, an employee's absence on maternity leave must not be excluded from her total length of service in respect of promotion or upgrading decisions.

Resignation

An employee who decides not to return to work after her maternity leave must give her employer notice of termination as required by her contract of employment.

Dismissal

If an employer refuses to permit an employee to return to work following maternity leave, this will amount to a dismissal in law. Such a dismissal will be automatically unfair. It is also automatically unfair to dismiss an employee (or select her for redundancy) during or at the end of her maternity leave if the reason for dismissal is that she took maternity leave. Such treatment is also likely to be regarded by an employment tribunal as unlawful discrimination under the **Equality Act 2010**.

Written statement of reason for dismissal

An employee who is dismissed (for whatever reason) either while pregnant, or at any time during ordinary or additional maternity leave, must be provided with a written statement explaining the reason for her dismissal. This rule applies even if the employee has not asked to be provided with such a statement and regardless of her length of service at the time.

Failure to provide such a written statement may lead to an award of compensation from an employment tribunal equivalent to two weeks' pay (which will be in addition to any other award of compensation payable in respect of the employee's dismissal).

Dismissal of a Replacement Employee

An employer that engages a replacement employee to fill in for an employee who is absent from work on maternity leave, must make it clear to the replacement employee, in writing, that he or she has been engaged for that specific purpose and that the employment will be terminated when the absentee employee returns to work. This type of contract will qualify as a fixed-term contract under the **Fixed-term Employees (Prevention of Less Favourable Treatment) Regulations 2002**. The dismissal of the replacement employee will be treated as having been for "some other substantial reason", which is a potentially fair reason for dismissal. There is no redundancy in these circumstances as the need for someone to do the job will not have disappeared or diminished. Provided the employer has properly notified the replacement employee that his or her employment will terminate when the absent employee returns, and acted reasonably in dismissing him or her, the dismissal will be fair. This may, however, be somewhat academic as employees need to have at least two years' continuous service in order to qualify for the right to bring a claim for unfair dismissal to the tribunal.

CONTRACTUAL MATERNITY RIGHTS

Some employers offer more generous maternity rights and benefits than those required by statute. Such enhanced rights are known as "contractual maternity rights". The most common ways in which contractual schemes enhance statutory maternity rights are where the employer allows periods of maternity leave that are longer than those provided for by law, and/or pays full or part salary rather than statutory maternity pay for all or part of the maternity leave period.

In these circumstances, the employee is entitled to select the most favourable terms, ie to "composite her rights". For example, if an employee is contractually entitled to a period of leave before and/or after giving birth that is longer than the 52 weeks of statutory maternity leave, she can still rely on her statutory right to return to work in the same job or a suitable alternative job after the longer period of contractual leave comes to an end.

Employers who grant enhanced contractual benefits to female employees on maternity leave may wish to consider granting employees on paternity leave and/or shared parental leave equivalent enhanced benefits. Adopting such a policy would fit in with an organisation's commitment to gender/diversity initiatives and commitment to family leave. It may also be advisable because it could potentially be argued that a policy of not granting men on paternity leave or shared parental leave the same enhanced benefits as are afforded to women on maternity leave amounts to unlawful sex discrimination (see below under *Shared Parental Leave*).

COMPLAINTS AND REMEDIES

Dismissal

The right to take maternity leave is enforced by means of an unfair dismissal claim to an employment tribunal where the employee is dismissed or selected for redundancy for reasons connected with pregnancy or the fact that she took, or sought to take, maternity leave, or where the employer refuses to permit the employee to return to work following maternity leave. No minimum period of qualifying service is required for this type of claim and such dismissals are automatically unfair. A complaint must normally be made to tribunal within three months of the effective date of termination.

Where a claim is successful, the employee will be awarded appropriate compensation for loss of earnings. The maximum amount of compensation payable to an employee who is unfairly dismissed or selected for redundancy for asserting his or her statutory right to shared parental leave is £78,335 (as from 6 April 2015).

There is a further cap on the unfair dismissal compensatory award equivalent to the claimant's annual salary. Thus, a successful claimant may be entitled to receive compensation for loss of earnings of up to one year's salary, or £78,335, whichever is the lower.

A failure to permit an employee to return to work at the end of maternity leave will, in most circumstances, also amount to unlawful sex discrimination. Where a claim for sex discrimination succeeds, compensation is unlimited and can include an award for injury to feelings.

Detriment

An employee is also protected against any detrimental treatment by the employer on grounds that:

- she is pregnant
- has given birth to a child
- has (while pregnant) been suspended from work for health and safety reasons without good cause
- has taken or sought to take maternity leave
- has refused to undertake work in respect of "keeping-in-touch days" during maternity leave.

"Detriment" is not defined in law, however a detriment will arise whenever there is any deliberate act or omission on the part of the employer which places the employee at a disadvantage.

In *Visa International Service Association v Paul* [2004] IRLR 42, for example, the employee brought proceedings of pregnancy-related detriment, pregnancy-related dismissal, unfair constructive dismissal and sex discrimination against her ex-employer. This was on account of the employer's failure to inform her of a new post while she was absent from work on maternity leave in circumstances where the employer knew that she had an interest in the particular type of work. When the employer brought a counterclaim seeking recovery of enhanced maternity benefits paid to Ms Paul, she brought further proceedings claiming that this action amounted to victimisation. It was not the employer's normal policy to seek repayment of enhanced maternity benefits in the event of an employee leaving the employment. The employment tribunal upheld all Ms Paul's claims and the EAT approved its decisions.

STATUTORY MATERNITY PAY (SMP)

Statutory maternity pay must be paid by the employer to any employee who is absent from work on maternity leave and who meets the necessary eligibility conditions and notification requirements for SMP. The employer can subsequently claim the majority of the payments back from the Government. SMP is payable whether or not the employee intends to return to work after maternity leave.

SMP is unaffected where more than one child is born as a result of the same pregnancy.

The period during which SMP is paid is known as the "maternity pay period".

Eligibility for SMP

In order to be entitled to SMP, a woman must:

- be engaged under a contract of employment (ie be an "employee" of the organisation)
- have been continuously employed by the employer for at least 26 weeks (irrespective of the number of hours worked), by the end of the 15th week before the expected week of childbirth (termed the "qualifying week")
- still be employed during either all or part of the qualifying week ("week" in this context means a week beginning with a Sunday)
- have weekly earnings averaged over the period of eight weeks up to and including the qualifying week (see below) which are equal to or higher than the lower earnings limit for National Insurance contributions' purposes (£112 per week as from April 2015)
- still be pregnant at the 11th week before the expected week of childbirth, or have given birth by then
- provide her employer with notice of her intention to take maternity leave and evidence of her expected date of childbirth
- have stopped work for her employer.

Where an employee works for more than one employer, she can receive SMP from each of them provided she meets the eligibility conditions set out above. Similarly, if she works under two or more separate contracts for the same employer and the earnings are not aggregated for National Insurance purposes, an entitlement to SMP can arise under each contract.

Where SMP is not payable

SMP will not be payable where an employee's contract has terminated before the beginning of the qualifying week, except where the employer has dismissed the employee solely or mainly to avoid SMP liability.

SMP can be paid only so long as the employee remains on maternity leave. If she elects to return to work before the end of the 39-week maternity pay period, she will lose entitlement to the remaining weeks of SMP. Similarly, SMP will not be payable for any week after the employee's confinement during which she works for another employer who is not liable to pay her SMP, and in any subsequent week during the maternity pay period.

Additionally, SMP will not be payable for any week in the maternity pay period in which the employee is detained in legal custody, or for any subsequent week. Where the employer believes that an employee is not entitled to SMP, the employer must provide her with certain information as she may be entitled to claim maternity allowance. Maternity allowance is a social security benefit payable to women who, due to short service, do not qualify for SMP but who satisfy certain conditions relating to National Insurance contributions on the basis of their previous employment or self-employment.

The employer must give the employee details of the decision not to pay SMP and the reasons for it within seven days of the decision being made or within 21 days of the employee giving notice of her intended maternity absence (if earlier).

Where SMP is no longer payable (for example, where the employee has been taken into legal custody), notification of this must be given to the employee within seven days of the employer being informed of the event that has caused the disqualification.

If an employee does not agree with the employer's decision not to pay SMP, she can make an application to an officer of the board of HM Revenue and Customs for a decision.

Calculating Average Weekly Earnings

The relevant eight-week period during which an employee's weekly earnings are averaged out for the purpose of calculating entitlement to SMP is based on the period which (working backwards) starts on the last normal payday before the end of the 15th week before the employee's expected week of childbirth, and ends on the last normal pay day falling at least eight weeks earlier than this.

It is important to note that the employee's average weekly earnings must be calculated to include all gross earnings derived from the employment. Such earnings must, therefore, include any overtime, commission and bonus payments that were paid during the relevant eight-week period.

Notification Requirements

In order to qualify for SMP, the employee must give advance notice to her employer of her intended absence from work due to pregnancy or confinement. This notice (which must be in writing if the employer requests it) must be given at least 28 days before the employee wishes her SMP to start, or, if that is not reasonably practicable, as soon as it is reasonably practicable.

The employee must also provide her employer with evidence of her pregnancy and the expected date of childbirth. This must be in the form of a certificate of expected confinement (normally Form Mat B1) issued by a doctor or registered midwife on or after the beginning of the 20th week before the expected week of childbirth. However, since the maternity certificate will not be issued by doctors until this point in time, employers may need to rely temporarily on other evidence to assist them to calculate an employee's eligibility for SMP subject to confirmation of the expected confinement date when the certificate is issued.

The requirement to give advance notification is modified where the employee gives birth earlier than expected. In these circumstances the employee must, within 21 days of the date she gave birth, give notice to the employer that her absence from work is due to confinement, and stating the date of her confinement.

Timing of SMP

SMP is paid to eligible employees for a maximum of 39 weeks (the "maternity pay period"). The maternity pay period is a flexible 39-week period which can start on any day of the week, but it cannot start before the beginning of the 11th week before the employee's expected week of childbirth. This condition applies regardless of whether the employee has remained at work up to this point in time. A pregnant employee may stop working at any time after the beginning of the qualifying week (the week that falls 15 weeks before the expected week of childbirth) and still be entitled to SMP when she reaches the beginning of the 11th week before the expected week of childbirth.

Rates of SMP

There are two rates of statutory maternity pay. For the first six weeks of the maternity pay period, the employee is entitled to receive the "higher rate", and for the remaining period of up to 33 weeks, a flat weekly "lower rate".

The higher rate is a weekly rate of 90% of the employee's weekly earnings, averaged over the period of eight weeks up to and including the qualifying week.

As from 6 April 2015, the lower rate of SMP is £139.58 per week. If, however, 90% of the employee's earnings is less than this amount, she will receive 90% of her earnings for the full 39 weeks of the maternity pay period instead of the higher rate followed by the lower rate. For example, an employee whose gross average weekly earnings are £150.00 per week would receive £135.00 per week as the higher rate (90% of her average weekly earnings) for the first six weeks of the maternity pay period. The lower rate applicable thereafter would also be £135.00 per week as this is less than the standard flat rate of £139.58.

Technically, SMP should be paid on the employee's normal paydays at the normal pay intervals. However, there appears to be nothing in the legislation preventing payment of SMP as a lump sum in advance, although this may in certain circumstances lead to an overpayment.

SMP is treated as earnings for the purposes of deductions for tax and National Insurance contributions.

Contractual payments made by way of remuneration or contractual maternity pay for any week in the maternity pay period go towards discharging the employer's liability to pay SMP.

The Effect of Pay Rises

Where an employee receives a back-dated pay increase which retrospectively affects her earnings during the eight-week SMP calculation period, her maternity pay must be recalculated and any arrears paid. Similarly, an employee who does not initially qualify for SMP due to her earnings falling below the level required (currently £112 per week) may subsequently become entitled to it as a result of a back-dated pay increase that brings her pay up to the required level. In this case, the employer must calculate and pay the employee the SMP due (offset against any contractual maternity pay she may have received).

Furthermore, as a result of a Court of Appeal decision (in *Alabaster v Barclays Bank plc* [2005] IRLR 576), where a pay rise is implemented at any time between the end of the eight-week calculation period for SMP but before the end of the employee's maternity leave (whether back-dated or not), this increase must be factored into the employee's SMP payments. This means that the employer must calculate, or re-calculate, the amount of SMP payable and pay the employee the difference between the amounts previously paid and the amounts actually due.

These provisions affect only the first six weeks of the maternity pay period during which the employee is entitled to be paid at a rate equivalent to 90% of her normal earnings.

Recovering Payments of SMP

Most employers are entitled to reclaim 92% of the amount of SMP paid from the Government, provided SMP has been properly paid.

Employers qualifying for small employers' relief can reclaim 100% of SMP paid out plus compensation amounting to a set percentage of the total SMP paid. The relevant percentage is deemed to be the broad equivalent of the total amount of secondary National Insurance contributions which are payable on SMP. The current percentage recoverable is 3% of the total SMP paid.

In order to qualify for small employers' relief, the employer must have paid (or be liable to pay) a total of £45,000 or less gross National Insurance contributions (employees' and employers' shares combined) in the last complete tax year before the beginning of the qualifying week (which is the 15th week before the employee's expected week of childbirth).

SMP is reclaimed by deducting the gross amount paid from the total amount of employees' and employers' National Insurance contributions for the tax month in which SMP was paid, or a later month. Where an employer wishes to recover SMP paid in a previous tax year, the Department for Work and Pensions should be consulted before deductions are made.

In order to justify reclaiming SMP, the employer must be able to show, if necessary to a DWP inspector, that the rules of the scheme have been satisfied. Employers must, therefore, by law, keep records showing:

- the dates of maternity leave notified by employees and, if different, the actual date of the first day of maternity leave
- the weeks in the relevant tax year for which SMP was paid and the amounts paid in each week
- the weeks within any maternity pay period for which SMP was not paid, together with the reasons for this
- maternity certificates or other medical evidence provided by employees to whom SMP was paid.

These records must be kept for at least three years after the end of the tax year in which the relevant maternity pay period ends.

Employers who produce false information in relation to the recovery of SMP will be liable on conviction to a fine of up to £5000 or a term of imprisonment of up to three months.

CHAPTER 2

PATERNITY RIGHTS

INTRODUCTION

Under the **Paternity and Adoption Leave Regulations 2002** (SI 2002 No. 2788), paternity leave is available to eligible employees where their partner gives birth to a child or adopts a child, provided (in the latter case) that the employee has not chosen to take adoption leave. Eligible employees are entitled to take two weeks' ordinary paternity leave, which must be taken within eight weeks of the date of the child's birth or adoption placement.

Under the **Work and Families Act 2006** and the **Additional Paternity Leave Regulations 2010** (SI 2010 No. 1055), employees whose child was due to be born or adopted before 5 April 2015 may also be eligible for additional paternity leave, provided they are still employed at the relevant time. The provisions for additional paternity leave are separate from and additional to the entitlement to two weeks' ordinary paternity leave.

Additional paternity leave is, however, being phased out in light of the introduction of shared parental leave (which applies to employees whose child was due to be born or adopted on or after 5 April 2015). The main provisions relevant to additional paternity leave are summarised in this chapter while shared parental leave is explored fully in chapter four.

Most employees who take paternity leave will be eligible to receive statutory paternity pay during their absence on paternity leave. Employers may recover most of this from the Government.

PATERNITY LEAVE

Entitlement

Paternity leave is available only to employees, ie those engaged on contracts of employment, and not to other workers such as contractors, temporary agency staff, casual workers or self-employed people.

Paternity rights are unaffected if more than one child is born as a result of the same pregnancy or more than one child adopted as part of the same placement.

An employee (whether part time, full time, permanent or temporary) will have the statutory right, subject to certain notification requirements, to take paternity leave if one of the following applies to him or her:

- he is the biological father of a child
- he is the husband or partner of a woman who has given birth to a child, but is not the biological father of the child
- she is the same-sex partner of the child's mother
- he is married to the child's adopter
- he is the partner or civil partner of the child's adopter
- he or she is one of a couple (whether male or female) who have adopted a child jointly and is not taking adoption leave.

Where a couple adopts a child jointly, one of them (the couple can choose which) will be eligible to take adoption leave while the other parent may be eligible for paternity leave.

In all cases, the employee must have, or expect to have, responsibility for the child's upbringing. It follows that paternity leave is not available to a man who is the biological father of a child but is not going to have parental responsibility for the child, for example, because he has separated from the child's mother.

Paternity leave can be available to a female employee in circumstances where she:

- is the partner of a man who has personally adopted a child
- is the partner or civil partner of a woman who has personally adopted a child
- adopts a child jointly with her husband or with a partner (whether male or female), and is not taking adoption leave
- is the same-sex partner or civil partner of a woman, or is married to a woman who has given birth to a child.

In all cases, there is a requirement for the employee taking paternity leave to have at least 26 weeks' continuous service, the timing of which varies depending on whether the leave is requested in respect of a birth child, a child adopted from within the UK or a child adopted from overseas.

Birth child

To qualify for paternity leave, an employee must have been continuously employed by his or her employer for a period of at least 26 weeks by the end of the 15th week before the mother's expected week of childbirth (termed the "qualifying week").

An employee will still be eligible to take paternity leave if the child is stillborn after the 24th week of pregnancy.

Child adopted from within the UK

The employee must have been continuously employed by his or her employer for at least 26 weeks by the end of the week in which the primary adopter was notified of having been matched with the child for adoption (termed the "relevant week").

Child adopted from overseas

The employee must have been continuously employed for 26 or more weeks ending with the week in which the primary adopter received official notification of acceptance for adoption from the relevant domestic authority.

Note: In a birth situation it is the mother's expected week of childbirth and not the actual date of birth, that determines the father's, husband's or partner's right to paternity leave. If the child is born early, this will not disentitle the father, husband or partner to paternity leave if he or she is otherwise eligible for it. Similarly, in the case of an adopted child, it is the expected (not the actual) date of placement that determines the right of the adopter's spouse or partner to take paternity leave.

Timing of Paternity Leave

Paternity leave (also known as "ordinary paternity leave") is a period of two consecutive weeks' leave which must be taken within eight weeks of the date of the child's birth or adoption placement. It is not permitted for an employee to take two separate weeks of ordinary paternity leave, and so if the employee elects to take only one week's leave, he or she may not take another week at a later date. Similarly, it is not open to an employee to take odd days of paternity leave.

Ordinary paternity leave must be taken in full:

- within 56 days of the child's birth or, if the child was born prematurely, within the period starting with the actual date of birth and ending 56 days after the week in which childbirth was expected to occur
- in the case of a child adopted from within the UK, within 56 days of the date on which the child was placed for adoption

- in the case of a child adopted from overseas, within 56 days of the child's entry into Great Britain.

Paternity leave can start on any day of the week but cannot begin before the date of the child's birth.

Where a child is born late, the employee must delay the start of ordinary paternity leave at least until the date the child is born. The eight-week period in these circumstances runs from the actual date of birth.

Notification Requirements

An employee wishing to take ordinary paternity leave must notify his or her employer of his or her intentions (in writing if requested), stating whether he or she wishes to take one week's paternity leave or two consecutive weeks' leave, and also stating the date on which he or she wants the period of leave to begin.

The timing of the notification varies depending on whether the leave is requested in respect of a birth child, a child adopted from within the UK or a child adopted from overseas.

Birth child

The employee must notify the employer of an intention to take paternity leave by the end of the 15th week before the mother's expected week of childbirth. The employee must also state the mother's expected week of childbirth (or, if the birth has already taken place, the actual date of the child's birth).

Child adopted from within the UK

The employee must notify the employer of his or her intention to take paternity leave within seven days of receiving formal notification of the match with a child for adoption. The employee must also state the date on which the adopter was notified of having been matched with the child, and the date on which the child is expected to be placed for adoption (or, if the placement has already occurred, the actual date of the child's placement).

Child adopted from overseas

The employee must notify the employer of his or her intention to take paternity leave within 28 days of receiving an official notification of acceptance for adoption by the relevant domestic authority. The employee must also state the date on which the child is expected to enter Britain.

An employee who has notified his or her employer of the date on which he or she wishes paternity leave to begin may change his or her mind about the start date, so long as he or she informs the employer of that fact and gives at least 28 days' notice of the revised start date or the original start date, whichever falls first.

In all cases, the employee must, if asked to do so by his or her employer, sign a declaration or self-certificate stating:

- that he or she satisfies the conditions of entitlement to paternity leave
- the nature of his or her relationship with the child and the mother (or adopter)
- that he or she has (or expects to have) responsibility or joint responsibility for the child's upbringing
- that his or her absence from work will be for the purpose of caring for the child or supporting the child's mother or adopter.

Employers may devise their own form of "declaration of family commitment" or they may require employees to complete and sign HMRC Form SC3, *Becoming a Parent* or SC4, *Becoming an Adoptive Parent*. Completion of the form is mandatory if, as is likely, an employee taking paternity leave also qualifies for statutory paternity pay.

ADDITIONAL PATERNITY LEAVE

Abolition of Additional Paternity Leave

Additional paternity leave, whose provisions are contained in the **Additional Paternity Leave Regulations 2010** (SI 2010 No. 1055), is being phased out following the introduction of shared parental leave (see chapter four). Employees whose child was due to be born or adopted on or after 5 April 2015 are no longer eligible for additional paternity leave, but may be entitled to shared parental leave instead. Additional paternity leave remains available for employees whose child was due to be born or adopted before 5 April 2015.

Note: It is the date on which the child was due to be born or adopted that is relevant and not the date the child was actually born or adopted (if that occurred earlier or later).

Entitlement to Additional Paternity Leave

Additional paternity leave is additional to and separate from the entitlement to the two weeks' (ordinary) paternity leave described above.

The conditions for eligibility for additional paternity leave are the same as those in place in respect of ordinary paternity leave, and so employees who are eligible for ordinary paternity leave are automatically eligible for additional paternity leave as well, provided they are still in employment at the time additional paternity leave is due to start and provided their child was due to be born or adopted before 5 April 2015. A further condition for eligibility for additional paternity leave is that the purpose of the leave must be to care for the child (not the child's mother).

Entitlement to additional paternity leave is contingent upon the mother of the employee's child or the primary adopter returning to work before the end of the period of maternity leave or adoption leave (52 weeks). Eligible employees can take between two weeks and 26 weeks' additional paternity leave in a single block. The leave may only be taken between the time the child is 20 weeks old and its first birthday and so it cannot be taken consecutively with ordinary paternity leave. In the case of an adopted child, additional paternity leave has to be taken within the period beginning 20 weeks and ending 12 months after the date of the adoption placement.

Because an employee can only take additional paternity leave if his or her spouse/partner has returned to work, it is not possible for both parents of the child to be on leave at the same time.

Despite the abolition of additional paternity leave in respect of births or adoptions which were due on or after 5 April 2015, the right for eligible employees to take additional paternity leave will continue throughout 2015 and into 2016. This is because up to 26 weeks' additional paternity leave can be taken up until the child's first birthday or the first anniversary of the adoption placement. Consequently, eligible employees may still apply for, and take, additional paternity leave through to April 2016, subject to the overall condition that their child must have been due to be born or adopted before 5 April 2015.

Notification Procedures for Additional Paternity Leave

An employee wishing to take additional paternity leave must provide his or her employer with certain information in writing:

- that he or she intends to take additional paternity leave
- the start and end dates of the proposed period of additional paternity leave
- a signed declaration confirming eligibility for additional paternity leave and stating that the purpose of the proposed period of leave is to care for a child
- the date on which the child was born or placed for adoption
- a signed declaration from the mother/adopter.

This information must be provided no later than eight weeks before the date on which the employee wishes the period of additional paternity leave to start.

Once an employee has provided proper notification of an intention to take additional paternity leave, the employer must respond in writing within 28 days, confirming the start and end dates of the period of leave.

An employee is permitted to change his or her mind about the start or finish date(s) of the period of additional paternity leave, provided he or she gives written notice of the proposed change at least six weeks before either the original start/finish date or the new date, whichever falls first.

Keeping-in-Touch Days

Provisions on "keeping-in-touch days" apply to employees on additional paternity leave in the same way as they apply to employees on maternity leave and adoption leave. Thus, employees on additional paternity leave may, by agreement, work for up to 10 days (either single days or combined in one or more blocks) without triggering the end of the period of additional paternity leave or losing any statutory paternity pay.

Rights if Job is Redundant during Additional Paternity Leave

An employee who is made redundant during additional paternity leave has the right (before the termination of employment under his or her existing contract) to be offered any suitable available vacancy that exists either with his or her employer or an associate or successor employer. This is the case irrespective of the fact that the employee may not be in a position to take up the new job straight away (eg he or she may have several months' additional paternity leave still outstanding). The offer must be made before the ending of employment under the existing contract and the new contract must take effect immediately on the ending of that contract. A "suitable available vacancy" is an alternative job which is:

- suitable and appropriate for the employee to do in the circumstances, and
- on terms that are not substantially less favourable to him or her than those of the previous contract.

Legislation requires that an employee on additional paternity leave must be given priority over any other redundant employees who are not on additional paternity leave (or maternity leave, adoption leave or shared parental leave) in respect of available suitable positions. This is the case even if the employee on additional paternity leave is not the best candidate for a particular vacant position — provided he or she meets the essential criteria for the post.

If there is no suitable work available for an employee on paternity leave whose job is redundant, the employer may lawfully terminate his or her contract on grounds of redundancy. In this case, the employee will be entitled to a statutory redundancy payment provided he or she has at least two years' continuous service, and possibly (depending on the terms of the contract) a contractual payment as well. Notice pay will also be due in accordance with the employee's contract.

Additionally, if the employee unreasonably refuses to accept an offer of suitable alternative employment, the employer may lawfully make him or her redundant, although in these circumstances the employee may lose the right to a statutory redundancy payment.

A failure to offer alternative employment to an employee on paternity leave whose job is redundant may be justified before an employment tribunal on either of the above grounds (provided the employer has the necessary evidence to present to the tribunal).

RIGHTS DURING PATERNITY LEAVE

Status of Contract of Employment

An employee on paternity leave (both ordinary paternity leave and additional paternity leave) has the right to the continuation of all contractual terms and conditions of employment, except pay (as is the case during maternity leave). Although not entitled to normal wages/salary (unless the contract states otherwise), the employee may qualify for statutory paternity pay (see below).

Accrual of Holiday Entitlement

Under the EU Working Time Directive (2003/88/EC), all workers must be granted at least four weeks' paid statutory annual leave. Under the UK's **Working Time Regulations 1998**, this period of annual leave was extended to 5.6 weeks (which may include paid public holidays). Many employers go further and grant their employees contractual holiday leave in excess of the statutory 5.6 weeks per annum.

Employees are entitled to continue to accrue both statutory and contractual annual leave throughout both ordinary and additional paternity leave.

RIGHT TO RETURN TO WORK

An employee returning to work after either ordinary paternity leave or additional paternity leave has the right to return to the same job as before on terms and conditions that are no less favourable than those that would have applied had he or she not taken paternity leave.

If, however, the employee takes a period of more than four weeks' unpaid parental leave in conjunction with paternity leave, the entitlement is to return either to the same job or, if it is not reasonably practicable for the employer to offer the same job, to another job which is suitable and appropriate for the employee in all the circumstances.

As notification of the start and end dates of additional paternity leave will have been given in advance of the start of the leave period, there is no further need for the employee to notify his or her return date.

Resignation

An employee who decides not to return to work after his or her period of paternity leave must give his or her employer notice of termination as required by the contract of employment.

Dismissal

It is automatically unfair to dismiss an employee (or select him or her for redundancy) during or at the end of ordinary or additional paternity leave if the reason for dismissal is that the employee took, or sought to take, paternity leave. A refusal to permit the employee to return to work following paternity leave also amounts to an automatically unfair dismissal.

CONTRACTUAL RIGHTS

Some employers offer more generous paternity rights and benefits than those required by statute. Such enhanced rights are known as "contractual rights". In these circumstances, the employee is entitled to select the most favourable terms, ie to "composite his or her rights". For example, if an employee is contractually entitled on the birth or adoption of a child to a period of leave that is longer than the two-week period of statutory paternity leave, he or she can still rely on the statutory right to return to work in the same job after that longer period of (contractual) leave comes to an end.

COMPLAINTS AND REMEDIES

Dismissal

It is automatically unfair to dismiss an employee (or select him or her for redundancy) during or at the end of paternity leave if the reason for dismissal is that he or she took, or sought to take, paternity leave. It is also automatically unfair to refuse to permit an employee to return to work following paternity leave.

No minimum period of qualifying service is required for this type of claim and such dismissals are automatically unfair. A complaint must normally be made to the tribunal within three months of the effective date of termination.

Where a claim is successful, the employee will be awarded appropriate compensation for loss of earnings. The maximum amount of compensation payable to an employee who is unfairly dismissed or selected for redundancy for asserting his or her statutory right to paternity leave is £78,335 (as from 6 April 2015).

There is a further cap on the unfair dismissal compensatory award equivalent to the claimant's annual salary. Thus, a successful claimant may be entitled to receive compensation for loss of earnings of up to one year's salary, or £78,335, whichever is the lower.

Detriment

An employee is also protected against any detrimental treatment by the employer on grounds that he or she has sought to take, or taken, paternity leave or refused to undertake work in respect of "keeping-in-touch days" during additional paternity leave. "Detriment" is not defined in law, however, a detriment will arise whenever there is any deliberate act or omission on the part of the employer which places the employee at a disadvantage.

STATUTORY PATERNITY PAY (SPP)

Statutory paternity pay (SPP) must be paid by the employer to any employee who is absent from work on paternity leave and who satisfies the necessary eligibility conditions and notification requirements for SPP. The employer can subsequently claim the majority of the payments back from the Government.

SPP is payable whether or not the employee intends to return to work after paternity leave.

SPP is unaffected in circumstances where more than one child is born or adopted as part of the same pregnancy or adoption placement.

The rules and eligibility requirements for SPP are similar to those applicable to statutory maternity pay (SMP).

Eligibility for SPP

In order to be entitled to SPP, the employee must be eligible for paternity leave and must, therefore, satisfy certain requirements as to his or her relationship with the person who is due to give birth to a child or adopt a child. The individual must be engaged under a contract of employment (ie be an "employee" of the organisation). He or she must also satisfy certain criteria related to length of service and earnings and must be absent from work on paternity leave.

Length of service

To be entitled to SPP, the employee must have been continuously employed by the employer for at least 26 weeks (irrespective of the number of hours worked per week) by the end of the "qualifying week" (birth) or the "relevant week" (adoption) and still be employed during either all or part of that week. "Week" in this context means a week beginning with a Sunday. The "qualifying week" is the 15th week before the week the child is expected to be born and the "relevant week" is the week in which the primary adopter is given notification of a match with the child for the purpose of adoption.

Over and above this length of service requirement, the employee must also continue in the employment up until the date the child is born or placed for adoption.

Earnings

The employee must have weekly earnings averaged over the period of eight weeks up to and including the qualifying week or relevant week which are equal to or higher than the lower earnings limit for National Insurance contributions' purposes (£112 per week as from April 2015).

It is important to note that the employee's average weekly earnings must be calculated to include all gross earnings derived from the employment. Such earnings must include any overtime, commission and/or bonus payments that are paid during the relevant eight-week period.

SPP for employees on additional paternity leave

With respect to employees who take additional paternity leave, statutory paternity pay is payable only if the mother or partner has a minimum of two weeks' unused statutory maternity pay or statutory adoption pay at the time of returning to work. Assuming this is the case, the mother's/partner's outstanding SMP or SAP is in effect transferred to the employee taking additional paternity leave at the same flat weekly rate. Since SMP and SAP are each payable for up to 39 weeks, employees taking additional paternity leave are eligible to receive statutory paternity pay only during this 39-week period. Any paternity leave taken beyond this period will, therefore, be unpaid (unless the employee's contract entitles him or her to payment).

Additionally, SPP can be paid only so long as the employee remains on paternity leave. If the employee elects to return to work before the end of the paternity pay period, he or she will lose entitlement to the remaining weeks of SPP.

Notification Requirements

In order to qualify for SPP, the employee must give advance notice to the employer of his or her intended absence from work on paternity leave. This notice (which must be in writing if the employer requests it) must be given at least 28 days before the employee wishes payment of SPP to start. If 28 days' notice is not reasonably practicable, notice must be given as soon as it is reasonably practicable.

Timing of SPP

The SPP commences on the day the employee begins ordinary paternity leave. It must end no later than eight weeks after the date of the child's birth or expected week of birth (whichever is the later), or the date of the child's placement for adoption.

As stated above, for SPP to be payable during additional paternity leave, the employee's spouse or partner must have returned to work within the period beginning 20 weeks and ending 12 months after the date of the child's birth or adoption placement and must, at that time, have a minimum of two weeks' statutory maternity pay or statutory adoption pay outstanding. Since SMP and SAP are each payable for up to 39 weeks, employees taking additional paternity leave can only receive SPP during the remaining portion of this 39-week period (ie the period that would otherwise have been the spouse or partner's 39-week maternity or adoption pay period).

Rates of SPP

The SPP is paid at a standard flat weekly rate. There is no "higher rate". As from 6 April 2015, the flat rate is £139.58 per week. If, however, 90% of the employee's earnings is less than this amount, he or she will receive 90% of his or her earnings instead. For example, an employee whose gross average weekly earnings are £150.00 per week would receive £135.00 per week (90% of his or her average weekly earnings) as this is less than the standard flat rate of £139.58.

The SPP is treated as earnings for the purposes of deductions for income tax and National Insurance contributions.

Recovering Payments of SPP

Most employers are entitled to reclaim 92% of the amount of SPP paid from the Government, provided SPP has been properly paid.

Employers qualifying for small employers' relief can reclaim 100% of SPP plus compensation amounting to a set percentage of the total SPP paid out. The relevant percentage is deemed to be the broad equivalent of the total amount of secondary National Insurance contributions which are payable on SPP. The current percentage recoverable is 3% of the total SPP paid.

In order to qualify for small employers' relief, the employer must have paid (or be liable to pay) a total of £45,000 or less gross National Insurance contributions (employees' and employers' shares combined) in the last complete tax year before the beginning of the qualifying week or relevant week.

The SPP is reclaimed by deducting the gross amount paid from the total amount of employees' and employers' National Insurance contributions for the tax month in which SPP was paid, or a later month. Where an employer wishes to recover SPP paid in a previous tax year, the Department for Work and Pensions should be consulted before deductions are made.

CHAPTER 3

ADOPTION RIGHTS

INTRODUCTION

Under the **Paternity and Adoption Leave Regulations 2002** (SI 2002 No. 2788), and the **Work and Families Act 2006**, an employee (whether part time, full time, permanent or temporary) who adopts a child, or who is one of a couple who jointly adopts a child, has the statutory right (subject to certain notification requirements) to take up to 52 consecutive weeks' adoption leave and resume working afterwards. The adopted child can be any age up to age 18. The legislation applies both to adoptions from within the UK and those from overseas, although there are different rules for each.

The adoption leave period is made up of 26 weeks' ordinary adoption leave and a further 26 weeks' additional adoption leave which begins on the day after the ordinary adoption leave period ends.

Most employees who take adoption leave will be eligible to receive statutory adoption pay for up to 39 weeks during their absence on adoption leave.

The right to adoption leave and the right to receive statutory adoption pay are contained in separate legislation and are based on separate criteria. To an extent, they operate independently of one another.

The legal framework for statutory adoption leave and pay largely mirrors that which is in place in respect of statutory maternity leave and pay.

Under provisions introduced by the **Shared Parental Leave Regulations 2014**, employees whose child was due to be adopted on or after 5 April 2015 and who have the right to adoption leave have the choice to end that leave on a date they specify and switch to "shared parental leave". This enables them to share the untaken balance of their leave and pay with their spouse, partner, civil partner or father of the child. Shared parental leave is explored fully in chapter four.

ADOPTION LEAVE

Entitlement

Adoption leave is available to an eligible employee (whether male or female and whether married, single, or a civil partner) where a child is matched or placed with him or her for adoption by an approved adoption agency. The child may be any age up to age 18. Since 5 April 2015, there is no minimum period of service required in order to be eligible for adoption leave (although there is still a requirement to have at least 26 weeks' continuous service in order to be eligible for statutory adoption pay – see below).

Adoption leave is also available to an employee who is one of a couple that adopts a child jointly. In this case, however, only one of the adoptive parents is entitled to take adoption leave, and the couple can choose which. The other adoptive parent may be entitled to take paternity leave if he or she meets the relevant criteria (see chapter two).

For adoption placements on or after 5 April 2015, eligibility for adoption leave (and pay) extends to prospective parents taking part in the "fostering for adoption" scheme, and also to intended parents in a surrogacy arrangement who have applied (or intend to apply) for a parental order.

Adoption leave is available only to employees, ie those engaged on contracts of employment, and not to other workers such as contractors, temporary agency staff, casual workers or self-employed people.

Adoption rights are unaffected if more than one child is adopted as part of the same adoption placement.

Surrogate Parents

As from 5 April 2015, revised legislation gives parents who commission a surrogate to have a child on their behalf, and who apply for a parental order, the right to adoption leave (subject to the rule that only one of the adoptive parents can take adoption leave). Under a parental order, a child born to a surrogate mother will be treated in law as the commissioning parents' own child.

An employee taking adoption leave may also qualify for statutory adoption pay, subject to his or her meeting the relevant eligibility conditions (see below).

A commissioning mother or father who takes adoption leave may also have the right (subject to certain eligibility conditions) to switch from adoption leave to shared parental leave, allowing him or her to share any outstanding leave (and pay) with his or her spouse or partner.

The woman who has acted as the surrogate mother will be entitled to maternity leave and (if eligible) statutory maternity pay in the normal way. The commissioning mother in a surrogacy arrangement does not, however, have the right to maternity leave simply because she will not have been pregnant.

Timing of Adoption Leave

Adoption leave is made up of 26 weeks' ordinary adoption leave followed immediately by a further 26 weeks' additional adoption leave. Additional adoption leave starts on the day after the ordinary adoption leave period ends. Adoption leave must be taken in one block; it is not permitted to take a period of adoption leave, then return to work, then take another period of adoption leave.

An employee may choose to start adoption leave on the date of the child's placement (whether this is earlier or later than expected) or from a fixed date which can be up to 14 days before the expected date of placement. Adoption leave can start on any day of the week.

Employees also have the choice to take their full entitlement of 52 weeks' adoption leave or to return to work at any time before the expiry of the 52 weeks (subject to notice requirements).

Notification Requirements

To exercise the right to adoption leave, an employee must comply with certain notification requirements. He or she must notify the employer that he or she intends to take either ordinary adoption leave, or ordinary and additional adoption leave combined, no later than seven days after the date on which notification was received from the adoption agency of the match with the child, or as soon as is reasonably practicable thereafter.

Notice can be given orally, but must be in writing if the employer requests it. Notice must:

- state the date the child is expected to be placed for adoption
- specify the date on which the employee intends to start his or her period of adoption leave
- (if requested by the employer) be accompanied by a signed and dated "matching certificate" from the adoption agency.

For overseas adoptions, an employee must inform his or her employer of his or her intention to take adoption leave within 28 days of receiving an official notification of acceptance for adoption from the relevant domestic authority and must, if asked, produce a copy of that notification. Once the child enters Britain, the employee must then give the employer at least 28 days' notice of the date on which adoption leave is to start, as well as evidence (in the form of a plane ticket or an entry clearance certificate) confirming the child's arrival.

Change of mind

An employee who has notified his or her employer of the date on which he or she wishes adoption leave to begin may change his or her mind about the start date, so long as he or she informs the employer of that fact and gives at least 28 days' notice of the revised start date or the original start date, whichever falls first.

Employer's response to notification

Once an employee has provided proper notification of the intention to take adoption leave, the employer must respond in writing within 28 days. Specifically, the employer must write to the employee acknowledging his or her intentions and stating the latest date on which he or she must return to work after adoption leave. This date will fall 52 weeks after the date the employee's adoption leave is due to begin. It is safe for the employer to assume that this is the date of return unless the employee has previously stated that he or she does not intend to take the full entitlement of adoption leave and has given an earlier return to work date. In these circumstances, the employee will still be entitled to change his or her mind regarding the return date simply by notifying the employer that he or she wishes to take the full 52 weeks' adoption leave entitlement. Alternatively, if the employee wishes to return earlier than the previously stated date, he or she must give eight weeks' notice of the earlier return date (see below).

If the employer fails to respond within 28 days and/or has not told the employee when he or she is due to return to work, it will not be possible to prevent the employee from returning to work early without having given the proper notice, nor will it be possible to discipline or dismiss the employee for failing to return to work on time.

RIGHTS DURING ADOPTION LEAVE

Status of Contract of Employment

An employee has the right to the continuation of all his or her contractual terms and conditions of employment, except pay, throughout both ordinary and additional adoption leave. Terms will include, for example, use of a company car, use of company mobile phone or laptop, health insurance cover and accrual of holiday entitlement (see below) that would have applied to the employee but for his or her absence.

There is no duty on employers to continue an employee's normal wage or salary during adoption leave (although statutory adoption pay may be payable – see below).

Accrual of Holiday Entitlement

Under the EU Working Time Directive (2003/88/EC), all workers must be granted at least four weeks' paid statutory annual leave. Under the UK's **Working Time Regulations 1998**, this period of annual leave was extended to 5.6 weeks (which may include paid public holidays). Many employers go further and grant their employees contractual holiday leave in excess of the statutory 5.6 weeks per annum.

Employees who are on adoption leave are entitled to continue to accrue both statutory and contractual annual leave throughout their periods of adoption leave. Where, due to absence on adoption leave, the employee has been unable to take all his or her statutory annual leave, he or she must be permitted to carry it forward to the next holiday year and take it during that year.

Keeping-in-touch Days

A provision introduced by the **Work and Families Act 2006** allows for "keeping-in-touch days" (KIT days) during an employee's adoption leave. This allows an employee on adoption leave to go into work for up to 10 days (which may be either single days or combined in one or more blocks) without triggering the end of adoption leave or losing any statutory adoption pay. This provision does not, however, allow the period of adoption leave to be extended beyond a total of 52 weeks. KIT days can only be worked by agreement, ie the employer cannot insist that an employee on adoption leave must come in to work, nor does the employee have any right to be offered any work. Where an employee works for part of a day, this counts as a full day for this purpose.

KIT days can, by agreement, be arranged for any type of work but will often be used to allow an employee to attend a training course, be present at an important meeting or simply to allow the employee to keep up to date with a particular job or project.

Where KIT days are arranged, the employer must agree with the employee the rate of payment for the days worked. The employee will be entitled to be paid under the terms of his or her contract of employment. Any statutory or contractual adoption pay may be offset against the payment made for the days in question.

Reasonable Contact

In addition to the provision for KIT days, employers are entitled to maintain reasonable contact with employees who are on adoption leave. This may, for example, be in order to discuss the employee's plans for returning to work or to provide him or her with an update on developments in the workplace.

Employees also have the right to make reasonable contact with their employers while on adoption leave.

Disrupted Placement

If, after an employee has begun adoption leave, the expected placement does not occur, the employee's adoption leave period ends eight weeks after the start of the ordinary adoption leave period. If the newly-adopted child dies or is returned to the adoption agency, the employee's adoption leave period ends eight weeks from the end of the week in which the death occurred or the child was returned to the agency, provided this period of eight weeks does not extend beyond the date on which ordinary or additional adoption leave would otherwise have ended.

RIGHTS IF JOB IS REDUNDANT DURING ADOPTION LEAVE

An employee who is made redundant during either ordinary or additional adoption leave has the right (before the termination of employment under his or her existing contract) to be offered any suitable available vacancy that exists either with his or her employer or an associate or successor employer. This is the case irrespective of the fact that the employee may not be in a position to take up the new job straight away (ie the employee may have several months' adoption leave still outstanding). The offer must be made before the ending of employment under the existing contract and the new contract must take effect immediately on the ending of that contract. A "suitable available vacancy" is an alternative job which is:

- suitable and appropriate for the employee to do in the circumstances, and
- on terms that are not substantially less favourable to the employee than those of his or her previous contract, including provisions concerning capacity and place of work.

Legislation requires that an employee on adoption leave must be given priority over any other redundant employees who are not on adoption leave (or maternity leave, additional paternity leave or shared parental leave) in respect of available suitable positions. This is the case even if the employee on adoption leave is not the best candidate for a particular vacant position — provided he or she meets the essential criteria for the post.

If there is no suitable work available for an employee on adoption leave whose job is redundant, the employer may lawfully terminate his or her contract on grounds of redundancy. In this case, the employee will be entitled to a statutory redundancy payment provided he or she has at least two years' continuous service, and possibly (depending on the terms of the contract) a contractual payment as well. He or she will also be entitled to pay in lieu of notice in accordance with his or her contract.

Additionally, if the employee unreasonably refuses to accept an offer of suitable alternative employment, the employer may lawfully make him or her redundant, although in these circumstances the employee may lose the right to a statutory redundancy payment.

A failure to offer alternative employment to an employee on adoption leave whose job is redundant may be justified before an employment tribunal on either of the above grounds (provided the employer has the necessary evidence to present to the tribunal).

RIGHT TO RETURN TO WORK

Where an employee chooses to return to work at the end of additional adoption leave, there is no duty to give any notice to the employer —

the employee may simply turn up for work on the appointed day. The employer may, however, use the "reasonable contact" provisions (see above) to discuss this matter with the employee.

If the employee is ill and so unable to return to work on the date he or she is due to return, he or she should notify the employer of that fact in accordance with the employer's rules in relation to the notification of sickness absence. The employee will then be entitled to be paid statutory and/or contractual sick pay in the normal way.

If an employee who was entitled to adoption leave is not permitted to return to work at the end of the relevant adoption leave period, or on a properly notified earlier date, he or she will have been effectively dismissed by the employer. Such a dismissal will be automatically unfair and the employee can bring a claim to tribunal irrespective of his or her length of service at the time.

Notice Requirement for Early Return

An employee who wishes to return to work before the end of additional adoption leave, or before a previously notified return date, must notify the employer of the proposed early return date at least eight weeks before the date in question. If the employee does not do so, the employer may delay the employee's return until eight weeks have elapsed or until the date on which the employee would otherwise have been due to return, whichever occurs sooner. In these circumstances, the employer is under no obligation to pay the employee until the full eight-week notice period has expired and he or she has returned to work. The employer may not, however, postpone the employee's return beyond the date that the employee's adoption leave would otherwise have expired.

An employee is also required to give eight weeks' notice if he or she decides to return to work later than a previously notified return date.

There is no limit on the number of times that an employee can change his or her mind as to his or her return date provided he or she gives the required eight weeks' notice and provided the return date falls before the end of the period of 52 weeks' adoption leave.

Rights on Return

Different rules are in place as regards an employee's right to return to work depending on whether he or she chooses to return at or before the end of the ordinary adoption leave period (ie having taken adoption leave of 26 weeks or less) or during or at the end of additional adoption leave (ie having taken adoption leave of between 26 and 52 weeks).

An employee returning to work before or at the end of ordinary adoption leave has the right to do so in exactly the same job as he or she occupied before the period of adoption leave began.

An employee who takes additional adoption leave is entitled to return to work either in the job in which he or she was employed before the adoption leave began or, if that is not reasonably practicable from the employer's perspective, to another job that is both suitable and appropriate for him or her to do in the circumstances. Any alternative job must be on terms and conditions no less favourable to the employee than those that would have applied but for his or her absence on adoption leave.

Furthermore, any general pay rise that has been implemented during the employee's adoption leave must be granted to him or her on return.

Where the employee returns to work having taken up to four weeks' parental leave immediately after the ordinary adoption leave period, the right to return to work in his or her original job prevails. If, however, the employee takes more than four weeks' parental leave immediately following on from ordinary adoption leave and if, at the end of that period, it is not reasonably practicable for the employer to permit him or her to return to the original job, the employer may offer suitable alternative employment on terms and conditions no less favourable to the employee than those of his or her original job.

Where an employee takes a period of parental leave (of any length) immediately after a period of additional adoption leave, the employer may reinstate him or her either in his or her original job or, if that is not reasonably practicable, in a similar job on terms and conditions no less favourable than those to which the employee was entitled in his or her original job.

Continuity of Employment

Since an employee's contract of employment continues throughout adoption leave for all purposes except pay, the employee's continuity of service is preserved for statutory purposes. In other words, the period of absence on adoption leave is counted when calculating the employee's total length of service for statutory purposes, such as the right to statutory redundancy pay.

Additionally, an employee returning from adoption leave must be permitted to return with his or her seniority, pension and other contractual rights as they would have been had he or she not been absent, irrespective of whether he or she took only ordinary adoption leave or additional adoption leave as well. In other words, the whole of the adoption leave period must be counted when calculating the employee's entitlement to service-related benefits, for example, the length of service required for a pay increase or for additional annual holiday entitlement. Similarly, an employee's absence on adoption leave must not be excluded from his or her total length of service in respect of promotion or upgrading decisions.

Resignation

An employee who decides not to return to work after adoption leave must give his or her employer notice of termination as required by his or her contract of employment.

Dismissal

If an employer refuses to permit an employee to return to work following adoption leave, this will amount to a dismissal in law. Such a dismissal will be automatically unfair. It is also automatically unfair to dismiss an employee (or select him or her for redundancy) during or at the end of adoption leave if the reason for dismissal is that he or she took adoption leave.

Written statement of reason for dismissal

An employee who is dismissed (for whatever reason) at any time during ordinary or additional adoption leave, must be provided with a written statement explaining the reason for the dismissal. This rule applies even if the employee has not asked to be provided with such a statement and regardless of his or her length of service at the time. Failure to provide such a written statement may lead to an award of compensation from an employment tribunal equivalent to two weeks' pay (which will be in addition to any other award of compensation payable in respect of the dismissal).

Dismissal of a Replacement Employee

An employer that engages a replacement employee to "fill-in" for an employee who is absent from work on adoption leave, must make it clear to the replacement employee, in writing, that he or she has been engaged for that specific purpose and that the employment will be terminated once the absentee employee returns to work.

This type of contract will qualify as a fixed-term contract under the **Fixed-term Employees (Prevention of Less Favourable Treatment)**

Regulations 2002. The dismissal of the replacement employee will be treated as having been for "some other substantial reason", which is a potentially fair reason for dismissal. There is no redundancy in these circumstances as the need for someone to do the job will not have disappeared or diminished. Provided the employer has properly notified the replacement employee that his or her employment will terminate when the absent employee returns, and acted reasonably in dismissing the employee, the dismissal will be fair.

CONTRACTUAL RIGHTS

Some employers offer more generous rights and benefits to employees who adopt a child than those required by statute. Such enhanced rights are known as "contractual rights". In these circumstances, the employee is entitled to select the most favourable terms, ie to "composite his or her rights". For example, if an employee is contractually entitled to a period of leave before and/or after the child's adoption that is longer than the 52 weeks of statutory adoption leave, he or she can still rely on the statutory right to return to work in the same job or a suitable alternative job after that longer period of (contractual) leave comes to an end.

COMPLAINTS AND REMEDIES

Dismissal

The right to take adoption leave is enforced by means of an unfair dismissal claim to an employment tribunal where the employee is dismissed or selected for redundancy for reasons connected with the fact that he or she took, or sought to take, adoption leave, or where the employer refuses to permit the employee to return to work following adoption leave. No minimum period of qualifying service is required for this type of claim and such dismissals are automatically unfair. A complaint must normally be made to the tribunal within three months of the effective date of termination.

Where a claim is successful, the employee will be awarded appropriate compensation for loss of earnings. The maximum amount of compensation payable to an employee who is unfairly dismissed or selected for redundancy for asserting his or her statutory right to adoption leave is £78,335 (as from 6 April 2015).

There is a further cap on the unfair dismissal compensatory award equivalent to the claimant's annual salary. Thus, a successful claimant may be entitled to receive compensation for loss of earnings of up to one year's salary, or £78,335, whichever is the lower.

Detriment

An employee is also protected against any detrimental treatment by the employer on grounds that he or she has taken, or sought to take, adoption leave or refused to undertake work in respect of "keeping-in-touch-days" during adoption leave. "Detriment" is not defined in law, however a detriment will arise whenever there is any deliberate act or omission on the part of the employer which places the employee at a disadvantage.

STATUTORY ADOPTION PAY (SAP)

Statutory adoption pay (SAP) must be paid by the employer to any employee who is absent from work on adoption leave and who satisfies the relevant eligibility conditions and notification requirements for SAP. The employer can subsequently claim the majority of the payments back from the Government.

SAP is payable whether or not the employee intends to return to work after adoption leave.

The period during which SAP is paid is known as the "adoption pay period".

Eligibility for SAP

In order to be entitled to SAP, an employee must:

- be engaged under a contract of employment (ie be an "employee" of the organisation)
- have been continuously employed by the employer for at least 26 weeks (irrespective of the number of hours worked) by the end of the "relevant week" (which is the week in which the employee was given notification of a match with a child for the purposes of adoption)
- still be employed during either all or part of the relevant week ("week" in this context means a week beginning with a Sunday)
- have weekly earnings averaged over the period of eight weeks up to and including the relevant week that are equal to or higher than the lower earnings limit for National Insurance contributions' purposes (£112 per week as from April 2015)

- provide his or her employer with notice of his or her intention to take adoption leave
- have stopped work for the employer.

It is important to note that the employee's average weekly earnings must be calculated to include all gross earnings derived from the employment. Such earnings must include any overtime, commission and bonus payments that were paid during the relevant eight-week period.

Where an employee works for more than one employer, he or she can receive SAP from each of them provided he or she meets the eligibility conditions set out above. Similarly, where the employee works under two or more separate contracts for the same employer and the earnings are not aggregated for National Insurance purposes, an entitlement to SAP can arise under each contract.

Where SAP is not payable

SAP will not be payable where an employee's contract has terminated before the beginning of the relevant week, except where the employer has dismissed the employee solely or mainly to avoid SAP liability.

SAP can be paid only so long as the employee remains on adoption leave. If the employee elects to return to work before the end of the 39-week adoption pay period, he or she will lose entitlement to the remaining weeks of SAP. Similarly, SAP will not be payable for any week after the adoption placement during which the employee works for another employer who is not liable to pay him or her SAP, and in any subsequent week during the adoption pay period.

Additionally, SAP will not be payable for any week in the adoption pay period in which the employee is detained in legal custody, or for any subsequent week.

Where the employer believes that an employee is not entitled to SAP, the employer must give the employee details of the decision not to pay SAP and the reasons for it within seven days of the decision being made or within 21 days of the employee giving notice of his or her intended absence on adoption leave (if earlier).

Where SAP is no longer payable (for example, where the employee has been taken into legal custody), notification of this must be given within seven days of the employer being informed of the event that caused the disqualification.

If an employee does not agree with the employer's decision not to pay SAP, he or she can make an application to an officer of the board of HM Revenue and Customs for a decision.

Notification Requirements

In order to qualify for SAP, the employee must give advance notice to the employer of his or her intended absence from work on adoption leave. This notice (which must be in writing if the employer requests it) must be given at least 28 days before the employee wishes SAP to start, or, if 28 days' notice is not reasonably practicable, as soon as it is reasonably practicable.

Timing of SAP

SAP is paid to eligible employees for a maximum of 39 weeks (the "adoption pay period"). The adoption pay period begins on the day immediately following the day on which an employee begins his or her ordinary adoption leave. It cannot start until the employee begins his or her ordinary adoption leave. An employee may choose to start adoption leave on the date of the child's placement (whether this is earlier or later than expected) or from a fixed date which can be up to 14 days before the expected date of placement.

Rates of SAP

There are two rates of statutory adoption pay. For the first six weeks of the adoption pay period, the employee is entitled to receive the "higher rate", and for the remaining period of up to 33 weeks, a flat weekly "lower rate". Prior to 5 April 2015, statutory adoption pay was paid at the lower weekly rate for the full 39-week period.

The higher rate is a weekly rate of 90% of the employee's weekly earnings, averaged over the period of eight weeks running up to and including the relevant week.

As from 6 April 2015, the lower rate of SAP is £139.58 per week. If, however, 90% of the employee's earnings is less than this amount, he or she will receive 90% of his or her earnings for the full 39 weeks of the adoption pay period instead of the higher rate followed by the lower rate. For example, an employee whose gross average weekly earnings are £150.00 per week would receive £135.00 per week as the higher rate (90% of average weekly earnings) for the first six weeks of the adoption pay period. The lower rate applicable thereafter would also be £135.00 per week as this is less than the standard flat rate of £139.58.

SAP is treated as earnings for the purposes of deductions for income tax and National Insurance contributions.

Contractual payments made by way of remuneration or contractual adoption pay for any week in the adoption pay period go towards discharging the employer's liability to pay SAP.

Recovering Payments of SAP

Most employers are entitled to reclaim 92% of the amount of SAP paid from the Government, provided SAP has been properly paid.

Employers qualifying for small employers' relief can reclaim 100% of SAP plus compensation amounting to a set percentage of the total SAP paid out. The relevant percentage is deemed to be the broad equivalent of the total amount of secondary National Insurance contributions which are payable on SAP. The current percentage recoverable is 3% of the total SAP paid.

In order to qualify for small employers' relief, the employer must have paid (or be liable to pay) a total of £45,000 or less gross National Insurance contributions (employees' and employers' shares combined) in the last complete tax year before the beginning of the week in which the employee qualified for SAP.

SAP is reclaimed by deducting the gross amount paid from the total amount of employees' and employers' National Insurance contributions for the tax month in which SAP was paid, or a later month. Where an employer wishes to recover SAP paid in a previous tax year, the Department for Work and Pensions (DWP) should be consulted before deductions are made.

In order to justify reclaiming SAP, the employer must be able to show, if necessary to a DWP inspector, that the rules of the scheme have been satisfied. Employers must, therefore, by law keep records showing:
- the dates of adoption leave notified by employees and, if different, the actual date of the first day of adoption leave
- the weeks in the relevant tax year for which SAP was paid and the amounts paid in each week
- the weeks within any adoption pay period for which SAP was not paid, together with the reasons for this
- evidence of entitlement to SAP provided by the employees in question.

These records must be kept for at least three years after the end of the tax year in which the relevant adoption pay period ends.

Employers who produce false information in relation to the recovery of SAP will be liable on conviction to a fine of up to £5000 or a term of imprisonment of up to three months.

CHAPTER 4

SHARED PARENTAL LEAVE

INTRODUCTION

Legislation introducing shared parental leave was brought into force in December 2014 in respect of employees whose child was due to be born or adopted on or after 5 April 2015.

Note: It was the date the child was due to be born or adopted that was relevant — not the actual date of birth or adoption placement (should that have occurred either earlier or later than expected). The legislation came into force by way of the **Shared Parental Leave Regulations 2014** which were made under the **Children and Families Act 2014** and subsequently inserted into the **Employment Rights Act 1996**.

The legislation gives employees who are eligible for statutory maternity leave or statutory adoption leave the right, subject to certain conditions and restrictions, to elect to end their maternity or adoption leave and share the outstanding balance of that leave with their partners as shared parental leave. The shared parental leave scheme does not give employees any additional entitlement to leave or pay. Instead it gives parents much more flexibility than is available under maternity and adoption legislation to choose how they share time off for childcare responsibilities in the first year after a child is born or adopted.

As is the case for maternity and adoption leave, the right to shared parental leave extends only to employees of the organisation and not to other workers, for example, casual staff, consultants or self-employed people.

Note: The scheme of shared parental leave has nothing to do with the entitlement under the **Maternity and Parental Leave, etc Regulations 1999** (SI 1999 No. 3312) for employees with a minimum of one year's continuous service to take up to 18 weeks' unpaid parental leave to care for a child. Parental leave is detailed in chapter five.

Employers can find further advice and information about shared parental leave and pay in the BIS publication *Employer's Technical Guide to Shared Parental Leave and Pay* (available at *www.gov.uk*); and in the Acas Guide *Shared Parental Leave: A Good Practice Guide for Employers and Employees* (available at *www.acas.org.uk*).

SHARED PARENTAL LEAVE

Entitlement

Under the shared parental leave provisions, eligible employees have the choice to switch from maternity leave or adoption leave to shared parental leave, which enables them to share the untaken balance of their leave (and pay, if they are eligible for it) with their spouse, partner, civil partner or the father of the child.

If there is more than one partner, for example, if a pregnant employee's partner is not the father of the child, the employee must choose which one of them she wishes to share the leave with. An employee cannot choose to share her leave with more than one person in respect of the same child. In the event that a couple's relationship breaks down after shared parental leave has begun, it is not permitted for a new partner to take over the leave. Furthermore, to be eligible for shared parental leave, the partner must, at the time of the birth (or adoption), live with the employee and the child in "an enduring family relationship" and expect to have a responsibility (or joint responsibility) for the care of the child.

An employee whose spouse or partner is not eligible for shared parental leave (for example, because he or she is unemployed) may nevertheless opt into shared parental leave — even though there is no-one with whom he or she can share the leave. An employee may elect to do this if he or she wishes to take discontinuous periods of leave interspersed with periods of work. In this context, the phrase "shared parental leave" may seem a bit of a misnomer.

In order to be entitled to shared parental leave, both the employee and his or her spouse or partner must meet certain eligibility conditions. For the employee, he or she must:

- be entitled to statutory maternity leave or statutory adoption leave, or
- be entitled to statutory maternity pay (SMP) or maternity allowance, in which case she can enable her husband or partner (or the father of the child) to take shared parental leave even though she herself may not be entitled to it
- have at least 26 weeks' continuous service as at the "relevant date" which falls at the end of the 15th week before the expected week of childbirth or (in the case of an adoption) by the end of the week in which the employee was formally notified by an approved adoption agency of the match with the child
- remain in continuous employment with the employer until the week before the start of shared parental leave
- have, or intend to have, responsibility (or joint responsibility) for the care of the child
- bring his or her entitlement to statutory maternity leave or statutory adoption leave to an end
- comply with certain notification requirements
- give his or her employer the child's birth certificate (or certificate of adoption placement) and/or the details of the other parent's employer, if requested.

Additionally, for the employee to qualify for shared parental leave, his or her spouse or partner must:

- have, or intend to have, responsibility (or joint responsibility) for the care of the child
- comply with certain notification requirements
- satisfy the "employment and earnings test" (see below).

For the employee's spouse/partner to be eligible to take shared parental leave, he or she must:

- have at least 26 weeks' continuous service as at the "relevant date" (see above)
- remain in continuous employment with the employer until the week before the start of shared parental leave
- have, or intend to have, responsibility (or joint responsibility) for the care of the child
- comply with certain notification requirements.

It can be seen from the above that, for there to be an entitlement for an employee to take shared parental leave in conjunction with his or her spouse or partner, both partners must have at least 26 weeks' continuous service with their respective employers as at the relevant date and remain in their employment until the week before the start of shared parental leave, and both must have, or intend to have, responsibility for the care of the child.

Employment and Earnings Test

For an employee to be entitled to take shared parental leave along with his or her spouse/partner, the spouse/partner must satisfy the "employment and earnings test". This requires the employee's spouse/partner to have been an employed or self-employed earner in Britain for a minimum of 26 weeks (which can be continuous or discontinuous) during the 66 weeks leading up to the expected week of childbirth or adoption placement. Additionally, the spouse/partner must have earned an average of at least £30 per week during at least 13 of those weeks.

This means that some self-employed people may be eligible for shared parental leave if their spouse/partner is employed and eligible for statutory maternity leave or statutory adoption leave. However, because self-employed people are not entitled in their own right to statutory maternity leave or statutory adoption leave, they cannot become entitled to shared parental leave other than in circumstances where their spouse/partner is eligible for statutory maternity leave or statutory adoption leave.

Timing and Length of Shared Parental Leave

Maximum period of shared parental leave

Provided both the employee and his or her partner meet all the qualifying conditions, they are together entitled to take up to 52 weeks' shared parental leave in total. The employee who is entitled to maternity leave or adoption leave has the right to give notice to end that leave on a specified date, and so allow the untaken balance of the leave to be shared with his or her spouse or partner as shared parental leave.

It is important to note that shared parental leave is not an entitlement that is additional to maternity leave or adoption leave — the legislation gives employees the choice to cut short their maternity or adoption leave and take the untaken balance of that leave as shared parental leave instead.

Timing

Shared parental leave is, technically, available from the date of the child's birth or adoption placement. For employees who give birth, however, shared parental leave can only be taken as from the beginning of the third week after the child is born. This is because the first two weeks starting on the day the baby is born are deemed to be "compulsory maternity leave" (**Employment Rights Act 1996, s.72**). For women who work in factories or workshops, the compulsory maternity leave period is four weeks (**Public Health Act 1936, s.205**).

Although a mother cannot switch from maternity leave to shared parental leave until at least two weeks after the birth of her child, her spouse or partner can give notice to commence his leave as from the date of the birth (provided the mother has given a valid curtailment notice to her employer and provided both parents have submitted notices of entitlement (see below) to their respective employers).

For parents switching from adoption leave to shared parental leave, the shared parental leave for either or both parents can begin at any time from the date of the adoption placement, subject to the notification requirements.

An employee does not need to have actually ended her maternity leave before her spouse or partner begins shared parental leave. Provided the employee has submitted a "curtailment notice" (see below) to end her maternity leave, her partner can start to take shared parental leave (subject to the requirement to give the necessary notifications to his or her employer) as from eight weeks after the curtailment notice was given. This means that the employee's spouse or partner could begin to take shared parental leave while the employee herself is still on maternity leave. The same principles apply to employees entitled to adoption leave.

Further rules are that:
- shared parental leave cannot be taken before the child is born or placed for adoption
- shared parental leave must be taken in complete weeks
- the minimum period of shared parental leave which may be taken is one week
- shared parental leave may start on any day of the week
- shared parental leave can be taken only up until the day before the child's first birthday or the date that falls one year after the date of the adoption placement
- any periods of shared parental leave that are not taken are lost because shared parental leave cannot be extended beyond the 52-week period beginning on the date of the child's birth or adoption placement
- shared parental leave may be taken as one continuous period or in discontinuous periods, subject to certain conditions and restrictions (see below for more details of continuous and discontinuous periods of leave).

The employee and the spouse/partner may elect to take shared parental leave concurrently or at different times from each other and may each, to a limited extent, stop and start leave to suit their individual circumstances.

Notification Requirements

There are three types of notice required of the employee and two for the spouse/partner in order for them to opt in to the shared parental leave scheme. All of these must be given in writing with a minimum of eight weeks' notice. The required notices are:
- a "curtailment notice" (mother or primary adopter only)
- a "notice of entitlement"
- booking notices (also known as "period of leave notices").

In order to activate statutory shared parental pay, separate notifications are required (see below).

Curtailment notice

The employee who is entitled to maternity leave or adoption leave must, first, give his or her employer a written notice of curtailment of maternity or adoption leave stating that he or she wishes to end that leave on a specified date (termed the "leave curtailment date"). The purpose of a curtailment notice is simply to shorten the amount of maternity leave or adoption leave available to the employee and allow the balance to be taken as shared parental leave instead.

For employees who give birth, the leave curtailment date cannot be before the end of the two-week compulsory maternity leave period (or the four-week period under the **Public Health Act 1936** for factory workers, where this is applicable).

The curtailment notice must be given at least eight weeks before the date the employee wishes the maternity or adoption leave period to end. Notice may be given more than eight weeks in advance. If, having submitted a curtailment notice, the employee returns to work before the expiry of the eight-week notice period, the amount of shared parental leave to which he or she will be entitled is reduced in accordance with the number of weeks between the return date and the notified leave curtailment date. For example, if an employee has given eight weeks' notice to curtail his or her maternity/adoption leave on 24 November, but he or she returns to work on 3 November, the amount of shared parental leave available to him or her and his or her spouse/partner will be reduced by three weeks.

As an alternative to submitting a curtailment notice, the employee may simply return to work early, ie before the end of the statutory maternity or adoption leave period. It should be remembered, however, that to return to work early from maternity or adoption leave, the employee must give his or her employer eight weeks' notice in writing of the early return date.

The curtailment notice must be accompanied by a "notice of entitlement" — see below.

Right to revoke a curtailment notice

A special provision applies in respect of employees who submit a curtailment notice before the child's birth. An employee who does this has a six-week period following the birth to change her mind about bringing her maternity leave to an end on the date specified. The employee has the right in these circumstances to submit a written "revocation notice" to her employer stating that she wishes to revoke her curtailment notice.

The employee may then, at a later date, issue a fresh curtailment notice setting out a new leave curtailment date, thus, allowing her and her husband/partner to opt into shared parental leave at a later time.

An employee may also withdraw a previously submitted leave curtailment notice if his or her spouse or partner dies, provided the revocation notice is given within a reasonably practicable time after the death.

Note: In these circumstances, however, the employee will not have the opportunity to opt into shared parental leave at a later date.

Additionally, a leave curtailment notice may be revoked within eight weeks after it was submitted if it transpires that neither parent is entitled to shared parental leave after all.

Note: That the right to revoke a curtailment notice applies only in the above circumstances. In all other circumstances, the curtailment notice, once given, is binding.

Notice of entitlement

Along with the curtailment notice, the employee must give a notice of entitlement and intention to take shared parental leave to his or her employer. The employee's spouse/partner must similarly give a notice of entitlement to his or her employer. The intention of the notice of entitlement is simply to give the employer an indication of the periods of leave that the employee is considering taking.

The rules for a notice of entitlement are that it must:

- be submitted at least eight weeks' before the start date of the first period of shared parental leave that the employee (or his or her spouse/partner) proposes to take
- be accompanied by a declaration from the employee and one from his or her spouse or partner (see below)
- state the names of the employee and his or her spouse/partner
- state the expected week of the child's birth or adoption
- state the actual date of birth (if the child has not yet been born at that point in time, this information must be provided as soon as reasonably practicable after the birth)
- confirm the start and end dates of any period of statutory maternity (or adoption) leave that has been taken or is still to be taken by the mother or primary adopter
- state the total amount of shared parental leave available
- state the total amount of shared parental leave that each partner intends to take
- set out an indication of the intended split of the shared parental leave between each parent
- give the start and end dates of the proposed periods of shared parental leave.

The intended split of leave and proposed dates of leave periods are not, however binding, ie the employee and/or the spouse/partner may choose different dates for their leave when they submit booking notices (see below) to their respective employers.

Within 14 days of receiving a notice of entitlement, the employer may request a copy of the child's birth certificate or adoption certificate and the name and address of the other parent's employer. The employee must then provide this information within 14 days of the employer's request. If the other parent does not have an employer (ie he or she is self-employed), the employee must confirm this in writing.

Declarations to support notice of entitlement

Both the employee and his or her spouse/partner must, when submitting notices of entitlement to their respective employers, include a declaration from each of them.

For the employee (ie the mother or primary adopter), the declaration must state that:

- he or she satisfies the conditions for eligibility for shared parental leave
- the information given in the notice of entitlement is accurate

- he or she will immediately inform the employer if he or she ceases to care for the child.

The accompanying declaration from the employee's spouse or partner must state:

- his or her name, address and National Insurance number
- that he or she satisfies the conditions for eligibility for shared parental leave
- that he or she is the mother or primary adopter's spouse, civil partner or partner or the father of the child (whichever is the case)
- that he or she consents to the amount of shared parental leave that the mother or primary adopter intends to take
- that he or she consents to the mother or primary adopter's employer processing the information in his or her declaration.

The declaration that the spouse/partner of the mother or primary adopter must give to his or her employer along with the notice of entitlement must state that:

- he or she satisfies the conditions for eligibility for shared parental leave
- the information given in the notice of entitlement is accurate
- he or she is the mother/primary adopter's spouse, civil partner or partner or the father of the child (whichever is the case)
- he or she will immediately inform the employer if he or she ceases to care for the child
- he or she will immediately inform the employer if the mother/ primary adopter tells him or her that he or she has revoked his or her leave curtailment notice.

The accompanying declaration from the mother or primary adopter must state:

- his or her name, address and National Insurance number
- that he or she satisfies the conditions for eligibility for shared parental leave
- that he or she consents to the amount of shared parental leave that the spouse or partner intends to take
- that he or she will immediately inform the spouse/partner if he or she revokes his or her curtailment notice.

Booking notice
Once the employee has submitted a notice of entitlement, the employee (and his or her spouse/partner) may submit written "period of leave notices" to their respective employers to book actual periods of shared parental leave. Such notices are also termed "booking notices". Booking

notices are an additional requirement over and above the curtailment notice and the notice of entitlement.

The first booking notice can be provided at the same time as, or after, the employee's "notice of entitlement" is submitted, but not before.

A booking notice can request either a single continuous period of shared parental leave or two or more discontinuous periods of leave. A "discontinuous period of leave" means a block of time containing two or more separate periods of leave interspersed with periods when the employee returns to normal working.

Each booking notice must be provided at least eight weeks in advance of the start date of the requested period of leave and must set out the intended start and end dates of the period of leave. Where the employee is requesting two or more discontinuous periods of leave in a single booking notice, the booking notice must be provided at least eight weeks in advance of the start date of the first period of leave and must set out the intended start and end dates of all the periods of leave requested.

Where a booking notice is submitted before the child is born, the employee may, if he or she wishes, specify that the start date of a period of shared parental leave will be the date the child is born or a specified number of days after that date; the end date of the leave period may also be expressed as a set number of days after the child's date of birth. These principles apply equally to eligible adoptive parents.

Variation notices

An employee may change his or her mind with respect to the dates of shared parental leave that he or she has requested by giving the employer a written "variation notice" which does one of the following:

- states the proposed new start date and/or end date of a period of previously booked shared parental leave
- cancels the period of leave previously booked
- asks for a single period of shared parental leave to be changed into discontinuous periods of leave or vice versa.

Variation notices, like booking notices, must be submitted with not less than eight weeks' notice.

Limit of three booking/variation notices

Both the employee and his or her spouse/partner are entitled to give three separate notices to their respective employers to book three separate continuous periods of shared parental leave, ie the original notification plus two further notifications or changes to pre-notified dates (ie "variation notices"). Subject to the employee meeting all the relevant conditions, this has the effect that the employee can, in practice, insist on three separate periods of leave broken up by periods of normal working.

A variation notice will, in most cases, count as a "booking notice" for the purpose of the limit of three booking notices that the employee is entitled to give. Where, however, the employee agrees to change the dates of a continuous period of shared parental leave as a result of a request by the employer, this does not count towards the limit of three booking notices. Any change that is agreed in this way should be confirmed in writing.

If an employee has more than one employer, the limit of three booking/variation notices applies in respect of each employer.

Early and late births

There is an exception to the requirement to give eight weeks' notice to vary the start date of a period of shared parental leave. The exception is where the child is born early, and the employee's shared parental leave (or her partner's) is due to start in the eight-week period following the week in which the child was expected. In these circumstances the employee and/or her partner may instead give notice "as soon as reasonably practicable" to vary the start date of the period of leave so that it begins the same number of days after the child's actual date of birth as it would have done after the expected date. So long as the length of the period of leave remains unchanged, the employer must agree to this type of variation.

For example, suppose the employee's child is expected on 5 October and both the employee and her partner have given notice to their respective employers that they want to take a period of shared parental leave commencing on 2 November and ending on 28 December. The baby is born two weeks early, on 21 September. Both the employee and her partner would have the right (if they wished) to submit variation notices to their respective employers to amend their periods of leave to start on 19 October and end on 14 December, and both employers would be obliged to agree to this provided the notices had been given as soon as reasonably practicable after the date the child was born.

Where the child is born later than expected, the employee and/or her spouse/partner may each, similarly, submit variation notices to their respective employers in order to amend the date on which shared parental leave is to start. Since shared parental leave cannot start before the date on which the child is born or adopted, the employer may (depending on the dates requested) have no option but to agree to this if the period of leave originally requested would otherwise be due to start before the child is born.

In both the circumstances described above, the variation notice does not count towards the limit of three booking/variation notices that the employee is entitled to give.

Notices that do not count towards the limit

Certain types of notice do not count towards the limit of three booking/ variation notices. The following acts as a recap of those that do not count towards the limit.

- A variation notice to change the start date of shared parental leave where the child is born earlier than expected, and where the period of shared parental leave was due to start within eight weeks of the week in which the child was expected.
- A variation notice to defer the start date of shared parental leave where the child is born later than expected and where the period of shared parental leave requested would otherwise start before the child is born (which is not permitted).
- A variation or withdrawal notice which is given in response to a request from the employer to vary the period of leave requested.
- A withdrawal notice where the employee's booking notice for discontinuous leave has been refused — provided the employee withdraws the booking notice on or before the 15th calendar day after the date on which it was submitted.

Responding to notices

Although there is no duty on an employer to respond formally to an employee's booking notice, it is good practice to do so.

If the employer does not respond to a booking notice requesting a single continuous period of shared parental leave, the employee will be entitled by default to take the period of leave requested.

CONTINUOUS AND DISCONTINUOUS PERIODS OF LEAVE

Continuous leave

"Continuous leave" means an individual period of leave, for example, eight consecutive weeks off work.

Subject to all the other relevant conditions, an employee (and his or her spouse/partner) who gives three booking notices (at different times) each of which requests a single continuous period of shared parental leave is automatically entitled to take these periods of leave. The employer cannot refuse requests for up to three continuous blocks of leave.

There is nothing in the legislation that would prevent an employer from discussing the dates of a period of continuous leave that an employee has requested with him or her. The employer is not, however, entitled to put pressure on the employee to change the dates notified in a continuous leave notification, irrespective of the perceived level of inconvenience or disruption that the employer believes the requested period of leave might cause.

Employers may lawfully refuse any requests for continuous periods of leave beyond three, although they may agree to further requests if they wish.

Discontinuous Leave

A "discontinuous period of leave" means a block of time containing two or more separate periods of leave punctuated with periods when the employee returns to normal working.

Employer's Right to Refuse a Request

Continuous leave
As stated earlier, an employer cannot refuse to agree to the first three requests from an eligible employee for a continuous period of shared parental leave. Once three booking or variation notices have been received, however, the employer may lawfully refuse a request for a further period of shared parental leave or for a variation to (or cancellation of) a previously notified period of leave. This is the case even if the employee and his or her spouse or partner have not used up their full entitlement to 52 weeks' leave. Employers may, however, agree to further requests if they wish, subject to the overall restriction that shared parental leave cannot extend beyond the date that falls 52 weeks after the date of the child's birth or adoption placement.

Discontinuous leave
Where a single booking notice specifies two or more discontinuous blocks of shared parental leave, the employer is entitled to refuse the request. In this situation, the employer and employee have a period of two weeks (14 calendar days) from the date the employee's booking notice was submitted to discuss the pattern of leave requested. This is

known as the "negotiation period". The employer may then agree to the leave requested, propose an alternative pattern of leave to the employee, or refuse the request.

Where no agreement is reached within the two-week negotiation period, or where the employer fails to respond to the request, or where a request for discontinuous leave is refused, the employee is entitled by default to take the total block of leave covered in the booking notice as one continuous period. The employee also has the right in these circumstances — within five days of the end of the two-week negotiation period — to nominate a later start date for the continuous block of leave. If no alternative start date is nominated, the period of leave will commence on the date that the employee proposed as the start date of the period of discontinuous leave.

The employee also has the option where a request for discontinuous leave is refused to withdraw the booking notice altogether, so long as he or she does so on or before the 15th calendar day after the date on which the booking notice was originally submitted.

Note: This type of withdrawal notice does not count towards the limit of three booking/variation notices that the employee is entitled to submit. Following withdrawal of the notice, the employee may submit a completely new request for a continuous block of shared parental leave or a different pattern of discontinuous leave.

It should be remembered, however, that because employees are entitled to issue three separate booking notices altogether, they have the right in practice to insist on taking up to three separate periods of continuous leave. Thus, although an employer has the option to refuse a request which specifies two or more discontinuous blocks of shared parental leave, it cannot refuse the first three requests for single periods of leave. Employees who wish to take shared parental leave in discontinuous blocks may, therefore (legitimately) act tactically and submit three separate booking notices (either at the same time or at separate times) each requesting a continuous period of shared parental leave — rather than submitting a single booking notice requesting discontinuous leave.

RIGHTS DURING SHARED PARENTAL LEAVE

An employee's statutory rights during shared parental leave are, essentially, the same as those that apply during maternity leave and adoption leave.

Status of Contract of Employment

An employee has the right to the continuation of all his or her contractual terms and conditions of employment, except pay, throughout shared parental leave. Terms will include, for example, use of a company car, use of company mobile phone or laptop, health insurance cover and accrual of holiday entitlement (see below) that would have applied to the employee but for his or her absence. Employees also remain bound by any obligations arising under their terms and conditions. The principles are the same as those applicable to employees on maternity leave or adoption leave.

There is no duty on employers to continue an employee's normal wage or salary during shared parental leave (although statutory shared parental pay may be payable — see below).

Accrual of Holiday Entitlement

Under the EU Working Time Directive (2003/88/EC), all workers must be granted at least four weeks' paid statutory annual leave. Under the UK's **Working Time Regulations 1998**, this period of annual leave was extended to 5.6 weeks (which may include paid public holidays). Many employers go further and grant their employees contractual holiday leave in excess of the statutory 5.6 weeks per annum.

Employees who are on shared parental leave are entitled to continue to accrue both statutory and contractual annual leave throughout their periods of leave. Where, due to absence on shared parental leave, the employee has been unable to take all his or her statutory annual leave, he or she must be permitted to carry it forward to the next holiday year and take it during that year.

Shared-Parental-Leave-in-Touch (SPLIT) Days

An employee and his or her spouse/partner may each attend work on up to 20 days (which can be either single days or one or more blocks of days) for training or any other work activity without triggering the end of shared parental leave or losing any statutory shared parental pay. These are termed "shared-parental-leave-in-touch days" (SPLIT days). If the employee works for only part of a day, that counts as one whole day for this purpose.

If an employee has more than one employer, he or she may work for up to 20 SPLIT days for each employer (subject to the relevant employer's agreement).

It is important to note that the employer cannot demand that an employee on shared parental leave must attend work, nor can the employee demand the right to work.

Where an employee works on a SPLIT day, the terms for attendance must be agreed between the employer and the employee. The employee will be entitled to be paid under the terms of his or her contract of employment.

Where the employee does work for up to 20 SPLIT days, this does not act to extend the period of shared parental leave.

It should be noted that the 20 SPLIT days are in addition to the 10 KIT ("keeping-in-touch" days) available to employees on maternity leave and adoption leave.

Reasonable Contact

Over and above SPLIT days, employers are entitled to maintain "reasonable contact" with employees who are on shared parental leave. This provision may, for example, be used to discuss the employee's plans for returning to work or to provide him or her with an update on developments in the workplace.

Employees also have the right to make reasonable contact with their employers while on shared parental leave.

RIGHTS IF JOB IS REDUNDANT DURING SHARED PARENTAL LEAVE

An employee who is made redundant during shared parental leave has the right (before the termination of employment under his or her existing contract) to be offered any suitable available vacancy that exists either with his or her employer or an associate or successor employer. This is the case irrespective of the fact that the employee may not be in a position to take up the new job straight away (ie the employee may have an entitlement to shared parental leave for several more months). The offer must be made before the ending of employment under the existing contract and the new contract must take effect immediately on the ending of that contract. A "suitable available vacancy" is an alternative job which is:

- suitable and appropriate for the employee to do in the circumstances, and

- on terms that are not substantially less favourable to the employee than those of his or her previous contract, including provisions concerning capacity and place of work.

Legislation requires that an employee on shared parental leave must be given priority over any other redundant employees who are not on shared parental leave (or maternity leave, adoption leave or additional paternity leave) in respect of available suitable positions. This is the case even if the employee on shared parental leave is not the best candidate for a particular vacant position — provided he or she meets the essential criteria for the post.

If there is no suitable work available for an employee on shared parental leave whose job is redundant, the employer may lawfully terminate his or her contract on grounds of redundancy. In this case, the employee will be entitled to a statutory redundancy payment provided he or she has at least two years' continuous service, and possibly (depending on the terms of the contract) a contractual payment as well. Notice pay will also be due in accordance with the employee's contract.

Additionally, if the employee unreasonably refuses to accept an offer of suitable alternative employment, the employer may lawfully make him or her redundant although in these circumstances the employee may lose the right to a statutory redundancy payment.

A failure to offer alternative employment to an employee on shared parental leave whose job is redundant may be justified before an employment tribunal on either of the above grounds, provided the employer has the necessary evidence to present to the tribunal.

RIGHT TO RETURN TO WORK

Employees have the right to return to the same job after any period of maternity, paternity, adoption or shared parental leave totalling 26 weeks or less in aggregate, even if the leave is taken in discontinuous blocks. This right is unaffected if the employee takes a period of up to four weeks' unpaid parental leave as well.

Where, however, an employee returns to work following a period of more than 26 weeks' leave in aggregate, or after a period of up to 26 weeks' leave combined with a period of unpaid parental leave lasting more than four weeks, the right to return is either to the same job or (if that is not reasonably practicable from the employer's perspective) to another job which is suitable for the employee, appropriate for him or her to do, and on no less favourable terms, including remuneration.

Notification of Return to Work

Since an employee on shared parental leave will have given notice of the start and end dates of the period of shared parental leave in his or her booking notice, there is no further requirement to notify an intention to return to work at the end of the agreed shared parental leave period. As noted above, however, either party may make "reasonable contact" during the period of leave to discuss the employee's return to work.

If an employee changes his or her mind with respect to the return date, he or she may submit a variation notice specifying an earlier or later return date. This variation notice must be given not less than eight weeks before either the original return date or the new return date, whichever falls first. Such a variation notice will count towards the limit of three booking/variation notices that an employee is entitled to submit.

Continuity of Employment

An employee returning to work from shared parental leave must be permitted to return with seniority, pension and other rights as they would have been if he or she had not been absent. This means that the whole of the shared parental leave period, together with any period of maternity or adoption leave taken, must be counted when calculating the employee's entitlement to service-related benefits, for example, the length of service required for a pay increase or for additional annual holiday entitlement. Similarly, an employee's absence on shared parental leave must not be excluded from his or her total length of service in respect of promotion or upgrading decisions.

CONTRACTUAL RIGHTS

Policy Matters

Following the introduction of shared parental leave, it will be important for employers to devise and implement a policy which sets out details of employees' rights. The policy should cover:

- statutory rights
- eligibility requirements for entitlement to shared parental leave

- what an employee needs to do in order to opt into the shared parental leave scheme and (where applicable) statutory shared parental pay
- any enhanced contractual rights available to employees, together with any conditions attached to these rights (see also next section)

The policy should cover both male and female employees and distinguish between employees who are new mothers or primary adopters (ie those eligible for maternity leave or adoption leave) and their partners. This is because the eligibility and notification requirements are different, depending on whether the employee who is opting into shared parental leave is the mother or primary adopter, or the spouse or partner of the mother/primary adopter.

Employers may also need to amend existing policies, eg those on maternity leave and adoption leave, in order to ensure consistency and completeness.

Discrimination in Contractual Rights

Employers who grant enhanced contractual benefits to female employees on maternity leave may wish to consider granting (both male and female) employees on shared parental leave (and/or paternity leave) equivalent enhanced benefits. Adopting such a policy would fit in with an organisation's commitment to gender/ diversity initiatives and commitment to family leave.

This may be advisable in any event because it could potentially be argued that not granting men on shared parental leave the same enhanced benefits as are afforded to women on maternity leave amounts to sex discrimination. In *Shuter v Ford Motor Co Ltd* ET Case No 3203504/13, Mr Shuter was paid the statutory rate of pay while on additional paternity leave, while female colleagues taking maternity leave were paid full pay. This was part of the employer's commitment to improve gender diversity as the make-up of the workforce was strongly male-dominated. Mr Shuter brought claims of both direct and indirect sex discrimination to an employment tribunal on account of this disparity. In respect of the claim for direct sex discrimination, the tribunal held that it was impermissible for a man on additional paternity leave to compare his treatment with that of a woman on maternity leave — the correct comparator was a woman taking additional paternity leave who, like Mr Shuter, would not have been entitled to the enhanced benefits.

In respect of the claim for indirect sex discrimination, the tribunal ruled that the employer's policy of providing full pay to women on maternity leave (but not to men on additional paternity leave) had a disproportionate adverse impact on men as a group, and put the claimant personally at a disadvantage. The claim failed only because the indirectly discriminatory effect was justified in the particular circumstances. The employer was able to demonstrate that the policy of paying enhanced benefits to female employees on maternity leave was appropriate and necessary with a view to achieving the legitimate aim of recruiting and retaining women in a strongly male-dominated working environment. The employer also produced evidence showing that this policy of enhancing maternity pay had actually resulted in an increase to the number of female employees in the workforce.

The *Shuter* case concerned an employee on additional paternity leave — which, in light of the introduction of shared parental leave, is being phased out (it is available only to employees whose child was due to be born or adopted before 5 April 2015). Additionally, the decision in this case was very fact-specific.

It is nevertheless possible that a claim for sex discrimination from a male employee could succeed in circumstances where an employer offers enhanced benefits to women on maternity leave but not to employees on shared parental leave. Although the Government has stated that it is not a legal requirement for employers to introduce enhancements to statutory shared parental pay for employees who take advantage of the shared parental leave scheme, this could be challenged in the courts. The position under the **Equality Act 2010** is not entirely clear-cut. Men can take shared parental leave from the date of their baby's birth and so the circumstances of a man on shared parental leave compared to those of a woman on maternity leave are much more similar now than was the case previously. It will ultimately be up to the courts to decide afresh whether it is permissible for a man on shared parental leave to compare his treatment with that of a woman on maternity leave, and it cannot be said with any certainty that such a comparison would not be permitted. It is technically possible that a claim for direct sex discrimination could be made out where employees on shared parental leave are not granted the same enhanced benefits as women on maternity leave.

Even if claims for direct sex discrimination in these circumstances were to fail, male employees on shared parental leave who are denied contractual benefits available to female employees on maternity leave could potentially make out a good argument for indirect (as opposed to direct) sex discrimination. They could argue that a policy of only granting enhanced benefits to women on maternity leave places more men than women at a disadvantage — simply because women in these circumstances would have the choice either to remain on maternity leave (with enhanced benefits) or switch to shared parental leave (without enhanced benefits) while men would only have the option to take shared parental leave (without enhanced benefits). Thus, a claim for indirect sex discrimination could possibly be established on the basis of disproportionate impact.

If this occurred, the employer would need to have objective justification for not conferring enhanced benefits on employees taking shared parental leave in circumstances where female employees on maternity leave were granted such benefits. In the Shuter case, the justification was based on the fact that the employer in question had a very low proportion of female employees and had proper reasons for wishing to encourage the recruitment and retention of women in the workforce in order to increase that proportion. That justification would not be available to employers whose workforce consists of roughly the same numbers of men and women.

Finally, it can be said with reasonable certainty that if an employer was to offer enhanced benefits to female employees switching from maternity leave to shared parental leave (perhaps in order to match enhanced maternity benefits), but not offer the same benefits to male employees taking shared parental leave, this would amount to direct sex discrimination. Shared parental leave applies equally to men and women and is aimed at equalising parents' access to leave; and so any unequal treatment of men and women on shared parental leave would almost certainly infringe the sex discrimination provisions of the **Equality Act 2010**.

COMPLAINTS AND REMEDIES

Dismissal

The right to take shared parental leave is enforced by means of an unfair dismissal claim to an employment tribunal where the employee is dismissed or selected for redundancy for reasons connected with the fact that he or she took, or sought to take, shared parental leave, or where the employer refuses to permit the employee to return to work following a period of shared parental leave. No minimum period of qualifying service is required for this type of claim and such dismissals are automatically unfair. A complaint must normally be made to tribunal within three months of the effective date of termination.

Where a claim is successful, the employee will be awarded appropriate compensation for loss of earnings. The maximum amount of compensation payable to an employee who is unfairly dismissed or selected for redundancy for asserting his or her statutory right to shared parental leave is £78,335 (as from 6 April 2015).

There is a further cap on the unfair dismissal compensatory award equivalent to the claimant's annual salary. Thus, a successful claimant may be entitled to receive compensation for loss of earnings of up to one year's salary, or £78,335, whichever is the lower.

If, however, a claim is one for unlawful discrimination, there is no cap on the amount of compensation that can be awarded, which can include an amount for injury to feelings.

Detriment

An employee is also protected against any detrimental treatment by the employer on grounds that he or she has taken or sought to take shared parental leave or refused to undertake work in respect of "shared-parental-leave-in-touch days" during his or her leave. "Detriment" is not defined in law, however, a detriment will arise whenever there is any deliberate act or omission on the part of the employer which places the employee at a disadvantage.

STATUTORY SHARED PARENTAL PAY (ShPP)

Introduction

Under the **Statutory Shared Parental Pay (General) Regulations 2014** (SI 2014 No. 3051), employees who switch from maternity leave or adoption leave to shared parental leave may, if they satisfy certain conditions, be able to share up to 39 weeks of statutory shared parental pay with their spouse or partner. Both the employee and the spouse/partner have to notify their respective employers of the amount of they intend to claim when they give notice that they intend to take shared parental leave.

Although ShPP is payable to eligible employees for up to 39 weeks, for employees switching from maternity leave to shared parental leave, the maximum that can be claimed is 37 weeks due to the two-week period of compulsory maternity leave (immediately after the birth) which an employee who has given birth cannot commute into shared parental leave.

Any weeks in which the employee has been paid statutory maternity pay or statutory adoption pay stand to be deducted from the total entitlement of 39 weeks' ShPP. The shared parental leave scheme does not give employees any additional entitlement to pay (or leave).

The employer's liability to pay ShPP ends when the maximum of 39 weeks' payment has been made. However, it can end earlier if the employee returns to work, begins work for another employer, is taken into legal custody or dies.

Eligibility for ShPP

The conditions for entitlement to ShPP for the employee who is the mother or primary adopter are that he or she must:

- have at least 26 weeks' continuous service as at the "relevant date", which falls at the end of the 15th week before the expected week of childbirth or (in the case of an adoption) by the end of the week in which the employee is formally notified by an approved adoption agency of the match with a child for adoption
- have average weekly earnings that are at least equivalent to the lower earnings limit for National Insurance contributions — currently £112 per week (as from 6 April 2015)
- have been entitled to statutory maternity pay or statutory adoption pay in respect of the child
- have submitted a pay curtailment notice to bring statutory maternity (or adoption) pay to an end
- still be employed by the employer in the week before the commencement of statutory shared parental pay
- be absent from work on shared parental leave (although the employee may do freelance or voluntary work without prejudicing the right to ShPP)
- have, or intend to have, responsibility (or joint responsibility) for the care of the child
- propose to care for the child during each week in respect of which statutory shared parental pay is paid
- comply with mandatory notice requirements.

In addition, for the mother or primary adopter to be entitled to ShPP, his or her spouse/partner must:

- have, or intend to have, responsibility (or joint responsibility) for the care of the child
- satisfy the "employment and earnings" test (see earlier in this chapter).

The conditions for a mother or primary adopter's spouse or partner to be entitled to ShPP are similar. He or she must:

- have at least 26 weeks' continuous service as at the "relevant date", which falls at the end of the 15th week before the expected week of childbirth or (in the case of an adoption) by the end of the week in which the employee is formally notified by an approved adoption agency of the match with a child for adoption
- have average weekly earnings that are at least equivalent to the lower earnings limit for National Insurance contributions — currently £112 per week (as from 6 April 2015)
- still be employed by the employer in the week before the commencement of statutory shared parental pay
- be absent from work (again, the spouse or partner may do freelance or voluntary work without prejudicing the right to ShPP)
- have, or intend to have, responsibility (or joint responsibility) for the care of the child
- propose to care for the child during each week in respect of which statutory shared parental pay is paid
- comply with the mandatory notice requirements.

In addition to the above conditions, for the spouse or partner of the mother or primary adopter to be entitled to ShPP, the mother/primary adopter must:

- have been entitled to statutory maternity pay, maternity allowance or statutory adoption pay in respect of the child
- have submitted a pay curtailment notice to bring statutory maternity (or adoption) pay to an end (see below)
- have, or intend to have, responsibility (or joint responsibility) for the care of the child, and
- satisfy the "employment and earnings" test (see earlier in this chapter).

Normal Weekly Earnings and the Lower Earnings Limit

To qualify for ShPP, the employee must have normal weekly earnings averaged over the eight weeks before the "relevant date" (see above) which are at least as much as the lower earnings limit for National Insurance contributions, currently £112 per week (as from April 2015). This is the same condition as applies in respect of eligibility for statutory maternity pay, statutory paternity pay and statutory adoption pay. It follows that if the mother of the child or primary adopter was entitled to statutory maternity pay or statutory adoption pay (respectively), it is likely that he or she will qualify for ShPP.

Employees who earn less than £112 per week may still qualify for shared parental leave, but they will not be eligible for ShPP.

Where, however, a woman is not entitled to statutory maternity pay because her earnings fall below the lower earnings limit, but is eligible for maternity allowance, she may give notice to curtail the maternity allowance and so create a right to ShPP just for her spouse/partner, even though she herself will not be eligible for it. Maternity allowance is a social security benefit payable to women who do not qualify for statutory maternity pay but who satisfy certain conditions relating to National Insurance contributions on the basis of their previous employment or self-employment.

Notification Requirements

In addition to the notices that an employee and his or her spouse or partner must give to opt-in to the shared parental leave scheme, there are two notice requirements that they must each comply with in order to be entitled to ShPP. These are that the employee must first submit a "pay curtailment notice" and thereafter both the employee and his or her spouse or partner must submit notices to claim ShPP.

Pay curtailment notice

In order to claim ShPP, the employee who is the mother or primary adopter must submit a "pay curtailment notice" in writing in order to bring his or her statutory maternity or adoption pay to an end and enable the remaining balance to be claimed as ShPP. The pay curtailment notice must specify the date on which the employee wants the maternity pay period or adoption pay period to end — which must be on the last day of a week (normally a Saturday). The pay curtailment notice must be given with at least eight weeks' notice. No other documents are required.

Normal practice would be to submit the pay curtailment notice at the same time as the leave curtailment notice (see earlier in this chapter).

It is important to note that an employee who wishes to share the outstanding balance of statutory maternity pay or statutory adoption pay with his or her spouse/partner must submit a pay curtailment notice — it is not sufficient to have submitted a leave curtailment notice or to have returned to work.

If, however, the employee submits a pay curtailment notice after having returned to work, the pay curtailment date will be the last day of the week in which the notice was given, irrespective of the date specified in the notice.

Right to revoke a pay curtailment notice

A special provision applies in respect of pregnant employees who submit a pay curtailment notice before the child's birth. An employee who does this has a six-week period following the birth to change her mind about bringing her statutory maternity pay to an end on the date specified in the notice. The employee has the right in these circumstances to submit a written "revocation notice" to the employer stating that she wishes to revoke her pay curtailment notice. This in effect cancels the pay curtailment notice.

The employee may subsequently, at a later date, issue a fresh pay curtailment notice setting out a new date on which she wishes statutory maternity pay to end. This means that the employee and her spouse/partner can subsequently opt into ShPP at a later time.

These provisions mirror those applicable in respect of curtailing maternity or adoption leave in order to opt-in to shared parental leave.

Note: This provision applies only in respect of employees who submit a pay curtailment notice before the child's birth unless the spouse/partner dies, in which case it can be revoked "within a reasonable period". In all other circumstances a curtailment notice, once given, is binding.

Notice to claim ShPP

Over and above the requirement for the mother or primary adopter to submit a pay curtailment notice, both the employee and his or her spouse or partner must give eight weeks' notice to their respective employers of an intention to claim ShPP. This notice can be included within the notice of entitlement to shared parental leave (see earlier in this chapter).

In order to claim ShPP, the employee (and his or her spouse or partner) must give the employer certain information in the notice, which includes:

- the employee's name
- the date the child is expected to be born (or adopted)
- the actual date of birth (if the child has not been born at that point in time, this information must be provided as soon as reasonably practicable after the birth)
- the total number of weeks in respect of which the employee is entitled to claim ShPP
- how many weeks of ShPP the employee actually intends to claim

- how many weeks of ShPP the employee's spouse/partner intends to claim
- the period(s) during which the employee intends to claim ShPP.

Each notice to claim ShPP must be accompanied by written declarations from both the employee and his or her spouse/partner. The signed declaration from the mother or primary adopter must state that:

- the information given in the notice to claim ShPP is correct
- he or she satisfies the qualifying conditions for ShPP
- he or she will immediately inform whoever is paying ShPP if statutory maternity pay, maternity allowance or statutory adoption pay is no longer being curtailed
- the date on which the maternity pay period or adoption pay period began
- the number of weeks by which the maternity pay period or adoption pay period will be reduced.

The signed declaration from the mother or primary adopter's spouse/partner must state:

- his or her name, address and National Insurance number
- that he or she consents to the mother/primary adopter's intended claim for ShPP
- that he or she satisfies the conditions required for the mother/primary adopter to qualify for ShPP
- that he or she consents to the processing of the information in the written declaration.

Rates of ShPP

ShPP is payable to eligible employees for up to 39 weeks at the flat weekly rate of £139.58 (as from April 2015). If, however, 90% of the employee's earnings is less than this amount, he or she will receive 90% of his or her earnings instead. For example, an employee whose gross average weekly earnings are £150.00 per week would receive £135.00 per week (90% of his or her average weekly earnings) as this is less than the standard flat rate of £139.58.

There is no "higher rate" as is the case with statutory maternity pay and statutory adoption pay.

For employees switching from maternity leave to shared parental leave, the maximum ShPP that can be claimed is 37 weeks due to the two-week period of compulsory maternity leave (immediately after the birth) which an employee who has given birth cannot commute into shared parental leave.

Note: An employee who is not eligible to receive ShPP may nevertheless be entitled to take shared parental leave. This could be the case where the employee earns less than the lower earnings limit for payment of National Insurance contributions.

Contractual payments made by way of remuneration or contractual maternity, paternity or adoption pay go towards discharging the employer's liability to pay ShPP.

ShPP is treated as earnings for the purposes of deductions for income tax and National Insurance contributions.

Recovering Payments of ShPP

An employer that has lawfully paid ShPP to an employee may claim back 92% of the amount paid from the Government by deducting the amount in question from the payments of employees' and employers' (combined) National Insurance contributions made to HMRC at the end of each tax month.

Employers that are eligible for small employers' relief may recover 100% of the amount of ShPP paid out, plus an additional amount in compensation (currently 3%) for the employer's portion of National Insurance contributions paid on ShPP.

In order to qualify for small employers' relief, the employer must have paid (or be liable to pay) a total of £45,000 or less gross National Insurance contributions (employees' and employers' shares combined) in the last complete tax year before the beginning of the week in which the employee qualified for ShPP.

CHAPTER 5

PARENTAL LEAVE

INTRODUCTION

The **Maternity and Parental Leave, etc Regulations 1999** (SI 1999 No. 3312) provide a statutory right for employees (both male and female) who have, or expect to have, responsibility for a child under age 18 to take unpaid time off work as parental leave for the purposes of caring for the child.

It is important to note that "parental leave", as described in this chapter, has no connection with and is completely different and separate from "shared parental leave" detailed in chapter four.

The right to parental leave is available to any employee (male or female) who has parental responsibility for a child under the **Children Act 1989** or **Children (Scotland) Act 1995**, or has been registered under the **Births and Deaths Registration Act 1953** or the **Registration of Births, Deaths and Marriages (Scotland) Act 1965**. This includes a parent (named on the birth certificate), an adoptive parent, or a person who has acquired formal parental responsibility for a child.

It is important to note that there is no entitlement for an employee taking parental leave to be paid during his or her period of leave, unless the employee's contract of employment expressly provides for a right to payment.

ENTITLEMENT TO PARENTAL LEAVE

The entitlement to parental leave applies to employees who have been continuously employed for at least one year.

The entitlement exists so long as the employee has parental responsibility for a child (including an adopted child) who is under 18 years of age. Up until 5 April 2015, parental leave could only be taken so long as the child was under five years of age (except in the case of a disabled child) or within five years of the adoption placement (or the child's 18th birthday if that occurred sooner).

The entitlement is to take a maximum of 18 weeks' unpaid parental leave in respect of each child.

RIGHTS DURING PARENTAL LEAVE

During parental leave, the employee's contract of employment continues to subsist, but not all its terms and conditions need to be continued.

The terms that continue are:

- the employer's implied obligation of trust and confidence
- terms concerning notice
- the right to redundancy pay in the event that the employee is made redundant (although this is subject to the employee having had at least two years' continuous service with the employer)
- disciplinary and grievance procedures
- the employee's implied obligation of good faith.

All other terms of the employee's contract, including pay, may be suspended for the duration of parental leave, unless the employee is entitled to continue to receive defined benefits under the terms of his or her contract of employment.

THE FALLBACK SCHEME

The detailed arrangements for the taking of parental leave may generally be agreed directly between the employer and its employees, or can be established through a workforce or collective agreement, provided that the agreed arrangements do not reduce the extent of employees' rights under the legislation. Specifically, it is open to the parties to agree arrangements for:

- the notice period required to take a period of parental leave
- postponement by the employer of a period of parental leave requested by the employee
- whether parental leave can be taken in a single period, in blocks of days or weeks, or in a combination of the two.

Where an employee's contract does not include any agreement on arrangements for parental leave or does not incorporate a workforce or collective agreement, the legislation provides for a "fallback scheme" to apply. The fallback scheme provides that:

- an employee may not take parental leave in periods of less than one week — except for the parents of a disabled child who may take parental leave in blocks of one or more single days
- an employee may not take more than four weeks' parental leave in any one year in respect of each child
- an employee must give his or her employer 21 days' notice of the period of parental leave he or she proposes to take and this notice must specify the dates on which the leave is to begin and end, or alternatively the duration of the period of leave
- the employer may postpone a period of parental leave requested by an employee for up to six months where the business would be unduly disrupted by his or her absence, provided written notice is given to the employee stating the reason for the postponement and specifying dates on which parental leave of the same length will be permitted.

Where an employer wishes to postpone the dates of an employee's parental leave, notice of postponement must be given to the employee no more than seven days after the employee's notice has been given to the employer.

Postponement of a period of parental leave cannot, however, be implemented where the employee's period of parental leave is timed to coincide with the birth or adoption of a child. In these circumstances, the employee has the absolute right to take parental leave at the time requested.

RETURN FROM PARENTAL LEAVE

An employee who takes parental leave for a period of four weeks or less is entitled to return to the job in which he or she was employed before his or her absence.

An employee who takes parental leave of more than four weeks is entitled either to return to the job in which he or she was employed before the absence or, if this is not reasonably practicable from the employer's perspective, to another job which is both suitable and appropriate for him or her to do.

In both cases, the employee's terms and conditions on return must be no less favourable to him or her than those that would have applied if he or she had not been absent on parental leave. Thus, the employee's seniority, pension rights and other similar rights must be at least as favourable as those that would have applied if he or she had worked normally during the period of parental leave.

COMPLAINTS AND REMEDIES

The right to parental leave is enforced by way of a claim to an employment tribunal. A claim may be brought on the basis that the employer has either prevented the employee from taking parental leave, or on the ground that the employer has unreasonably postponed a period of parental leave requested by the employee.

Where a tribunal finds a complaint well-founded, it must make a declaration to that effect and may award compensation to be paid to the employee in an amount that it considers to be just and equitable.

An employee who takes parental leave also has the right not to be subjected to any detriment or to be dismissed on account of having applied for, or taken, parental leave. No minimum period of qualifying service is required for this type of claim and such dismissals are automatically unfair. A complaint must normally be made to tribunal within three months of the effective date of termination.

CHAPTER 6

TIME OFF RIGHTS

INTRODUCTION

This chapter explores the rights of employees to take time off work for certain family-related reasons. Specifically, the text includes details of the right to:

- time off for antenatal care
- time off for pre-adoption appointments
- time off to accompany a spouse/partner to antenatal or pre-adoption appointments
- time off to care for dependants.

TIME OFF FOR ANTENATAL CARE

Employees who are pregnant have the right to take reasonable time off work on full pay for antenatal care. There is no length of service qualification for this right and the right applies irrespective of the number of hours the employee works.

"Antenatal care" is not defined but is likely to include (for example) relaxation classes — although this is a matter of some contention. In *Gregory v Tudsbury Ltd* [1982] IRLR 267, an employment tribunal accepted, with supporting medical evidence, that the relaxation classes the employee attended were an essential part of her antenatal care and so she was entitled to paid time off to attend them. In *Bateman v Flexible Lamps Ltd* ET Case No 3204707, however, a tribunal refused to accept that antenatal care would include parent-craft classes, describing them as merely optional.

Temporary agency staff who have worked for at least 12 weeks in the same role with the same organisation are also entitled to paid time off work to attend antenatal appointments. For permanent employees, there is no minimum period of qualifying service.

To be entitled to take time off for antenatal care, the employee must (if requested by the employer) produce a certificate of pregnancy and an appointment card, or some other documentary proof that the appointment has been made. This condition does not, however, apply to the first antenatal appointment. The appointment must have been made on the advice of a registered medical practitioner, registered midwife or registered nurse.

An employee taking time off for antenatal care is entitled to be paid her normal rate of pay while absent from work.

Amount of Time Off

An employer is only obliged to allow time off for antenatal care where it is "reasonable". "Reasonable" is not defined, however, what is reasonable in practice is likely to depend on the amount of time off needed, the frequency of requests, the amount of time off which has already been taken and the effects of the employee's absence on the employer. It would not, however, be advisable for an employer to refuse an employee time off for antenatal care as a refusal could risk being in breach of equality law and the common law duty of care.

For each appointment, the maximum amount of time off that may be taken is six and a half hours. The time off granted must include the time taken to travel to and from the place of the appointment.

It is not permitted for an employer to require an employee to work additional hours in order to make up the time spent travelling to or attending antenatal appointments. The right is to take time off during working hours. This also has the effect that an employer cannot insist that an employee (for example, a part-timer) must arrange her antenatal appointments at times when she is not rostered to work. This may in any event not be possible or practicable, as a clinic or class may take place on a set day of the week and at a set time.

IVF Treatment

There is no statutory right for an employee to take time off work for infertility investigations or IVF treatment. Employers should deal with requests for time off for appointments made in connection with IVF treatment in the same way as they would deal with requests for any other medical appointment.

Similarly, there is no statutory right to time off for pregnancy tests.

If an employee becomes ill as a result of IVF treatment, she will be entitled to statutory and/or contractual sick pay in the usual way.

TIME OFF FOR PRE-ADOPTION APPOINTMENTS

As from 5 April 2015, there is a right for an employee who is adopting a child (of up to age 18) to take time off to attend adoption appointments in advance of the child being placed for adoption. Where a couple adopt a child jointly, this right applies only in respect of one of the parents (the "primary adopter"). In this case, the other parent will be entitled to unpaid time off to accompany the primary adopter — see next section.

The right for an employee who is adopting a child is to take paid time off work for up to five pre-adoption appointments. The maximum amount of time off that may be taken for each appointment is six and a half hours and the time off granted must include the time taken to travel to and from the place of the appointment. There is no length of service qualification for this right and the right applies irrespective of the number of hours the employee works.

TIME OFF TO ACCOMPANY A SPOUSE/PARTNER TO ANTENATAL OR PRE-ADOPTION APPOINTMENTS

As from 1 October 2014, an employee who is the husband, partner or civil partner of a pregnant woman, or the father of the expected child, has the right to take unpaid time off during working hours to accompany the pregnant woman to up to two antenatal care appointments. This right also applies to intended parents in a surrogacy arrangement, ie one of the commissioning parents may accompany the pregnant surrogate to an appointment. There is no length of service requirement for this right and the right applies irrespective of the number of hours the employee works.

The maximum amount of time off that may be taken for each appointment is six and a half hours and the time off granted must include the time taken to travel to and from the place of the appointment.

For the right to time off to arise, the appointment must have been made on the advice of a registered medical practitioner, registered midwife or health visitor (as is the case in respect of pregnant employees' right to time off for antenatal care).

As from 5 April 2015, there is a right for adopters (see previous section) and their spouses/partners to take time off to attend adoption appointments in advance of a child being placed with them for adoption.

For the spouse/partner of the primary adopter, the right is to take unpaid time off work to accompany the primary adopter to up to two appointments.

There is no length of service qualification for these rights and the right applies irrespective of the number of hours the employee works.

TIME OFF TO CARE FOR DEPENDANTS

Introduction

Under s.57A of the **Employment Rights Act 1996**, employees have the right to take a reasonable amount of time off during working hours in order to deal with emergencies involving dependants. There is no statutory obligation on the employer to pay an employee for such time off, although a right to payment may arise under the employee's contract of employment.

The right to take time off work arises whenever it is necessary for an employee to take action in order:

- to provide assistance when a dependant falls ill, gives birth or is injured or assaulted
- to make arrangements for the provision of care of a dependant who has fallen ill or been injured
- as a consequence of the death of a dependant
- because of unexpected disruption or termination of arrangements for a dependant's care (for example, if an employee's childcare arrangements have unexpectedly broken down)
- to deal with an incident involving a child which occurs unexpectedly while the child is at school.

The right to time off to care for dependants is available to all employees irrespective of their length of service.

The employee is only entitled to time off to care for a dependant if he or she informs the employer as soon as is reasonably practicable:

- of the reason for the absence
- how long he or she expects the absence to last (except in cases where the employee is unable to inform the employer about the absence until he or she returns to work).

Definition of "Dependants"

The right to time off arises only in respect of situations affecting "dependants". In relation to an employee, a dependant is defined as a spouse, child, parent, or a person who lives in the same household as the employee other than a tenant, lodger, boarder or employee. This would include an unmarried partner of either sex, and (for example) an elderly relative.

Additionally, in a case involving illness or injury, "dependant" also includes anyone who reasonably relies on the employee for assistance or care, for example, an elderly neighbour.

The Scope of the Right to Time Off

The right to time off for dependants is not intended to give employees the right to take extended periods of time off work to care personally for a dependant, rather the right is to take a short period of time off to make arrangements for the dependant's care.

This distinction was demonstrated in the case of *Qua v John Ford Morrison Solicitors* [2003] IRLR 184. The employee had taken a total of 17 days off work in respect of her son's medical condition. The EAT stressed that the right to take time off to care for dependants is concerned with unexpected and unforeseeable events and the law does not grant employees a right to time off beyond that which is reasonable or necessary to deal with the immediate crisis. Thus, in relation to a child who is sick on repeated occasions, the employee does not have the right to take time off repeatedly in order personally to provide long-term care for the child — because the child's illness would, in these circumstances, not always be unforeseeable. Instead, the employee's right is to take a reasonable amount of time off work to make the necessary arrangements for the child's long-term care.

The EAT also commented that whether time off is "necessary" in the context of a dependant's illness would be contingent on the relationship between the employee and the dependant, the extent to which anyone else could provide assistance and the nature of the specific occurrence. How much time off is "reasonable" would depend on the circumstances of the individual employee and the number, length and dates of previous absences. The amount of inconvenience or disruption caused to the employer by the employee's absences would, however, be irrelevant to the judgment of how much time off was reasonable.

The right to time off to care for dependants is not intended to provide employees with a right to compassionate leave in the case of a bereavement. In *Forster v Cartwright Black Solicitors* [2004] IRLR 781, Ms Forster lost both her parents over a relatively short period of time. She had been granted 12 days' paid bereavement leave following the death of her father and, after her mother died four months later, she was granted five days' bereavement leave and was thereafter signed off sick for four weeks on account of the emotional effects of the bereavement.

Having been subsequently dismissed on account of her absence record, Ms Forster claimed that the reason for her dismissal was that she had taken "time off in consequence of the death of a dependant" as defined in the legislation, and that her dismissal was, therefore, automatically unfair.

The EAT ruled that the right to time off in consequence of the death of a dependant must be restricted to time off that is necessary as a result of the death, ie the time needed for the employee to deal with the direct consequences of the death, such as seeing to the legal matters and arranging and attending the funeral. The right to time off was not intended to include a period of compassionate leave for the bereaved employee.

In another case (*Royal Bank of Scotland plc v Harrison* EAT [2008] 0093/08), the EAT ruled that where the disruption to the arrangements for a dependant's care is unexpected, but not sudden, protection against detriment is not necessarily lost. The EAT stated that the key question was whether it was "necessary" for an employee to take time off work as a result of the disruption to care arrangements. Although the length of time between learning of a risk of disruption to arrangements and the risk becoming a reality was relevant to the question of whether time off work was necessary, there are, the EAT held, no hard and fast rules and each case stands to be considered on its own facts.

Duty to Notify the Employer

The right to take time off work to care for a dependant does not apply unless the employee notifies the employer of the reason for his or her absence as soon as is reasonably practicable and tells the employer for how long he or she expects to be absent. There is an exception to the latter where the employee has been unable to notify the employer of the likely length of his or her absence until he or she has returned to work.

These provisions clearly distinguish between cases where an employee has some advance knowledge of a particular situation, in which case the employer can legitimately expect some warning of the need for time off and the amount of time required, and emergencies or other situations where it is not possible for the employee to notify the employer in advance.

Amount of Time Off

The amount of time off that an employer must permit is that which is "reasonable". This will depend on the circumstances in which the employee needs to provide assistance or care, the degree of assistance or care which needs to be provided and the individual situation of the employee.

As detailed above, the EAT ruled in *Qua v John Ford Morrison Solicitors* [2003] IRLR 184 that the question of how much time off is "reasonable" will also depend on the circumstances of the individual employee and the number, length and dates of any previous absences.

Protection against Detriment and Dismissal

Employees who take time off work to care for a dependant have the right not to be subjected to any detriment or to be dismissed on account of having taken such time off.

If, however, an employee fails without good reason to notify his or her employer of the reason for his or her absence and/or how long he or she expects to be off work, protection against detriment or dismissal for taking the time off is likely to be lost.

In *Ellis v Ratcliff Palfinger Ltd* EAT 0438/13, for example, Mr Ellis, who was already subject to two written warnings, took the day off work to take his partner (who was heavily pregnant) to hospital. He did not, however, contact his employer to explain his absence. The next day the baby was born and Mr Ellis again did not attend work, nor did he make contact with the employer. He did not return to work until the following Monday.

Following a disciplinary hearing, the employer concluded that Mr Ellis had failed without good reason to keep management informed about his absence and when he was likely to return to work and, taking into account the earlier disciplinary warnings, dismissed him. He brought a claim of unfair dismissal to the tribunal, arguing that the dismissal was automatically unfair because the reason for it was that he had exercised his right to take time off to care for a dependant.

The EAT held that the right to time off was not engaged because Mr Ellis had failed, as required by the legislation, to inform his employer of the reason for his absence, nor had he let the employer know the expected duration of his absence. Mr Ellis had therefore not been automatically unfairly dismissed for exercising his right to take time off for dependants, rather he had been fairly dismissed for misconduct.

Complaints and Remedies

Where an employee is unreasonably refused time off to care for dependants, he or she may bring a complaint to an employment tribunal. A complaint must normally be made within three months of the date when the employer refused the time off. Where a tribunal decides that the complaint is well-founded, it will make a declaration to that effect and may award the employee compensation in an amount that it considers just and equitable in all the circumstances, taking into account the employer's fault and the employee's loss.

If an employee is dismissed, selected for redundancy or subjected to any type of detriment for asserting the right to time off to care for dependants, he or she may also complain to an employment tribunal. No qualifying period of service is needed to bring such a claim and no upper age limit applies. Once again, there is a three-month time limit for bringing the complaint to the tribunal which, in the case of dismissal, runs from the effective date of termination.

Such dismissals will be automatically unfair. For example, in *RKS Services v Palen* [2007] EAT 0300/06, the claimant, a delivery driver in a small company, was dismissed during his second week of employment when he took a day off work to care for his partner who had been taken ill. Although he did not have the necessary length of service to claim unfair dismissal in the normal way, he brought a claim asserting that the reason for his dismissal was that he had taken time off work to care for dependants. The tribunal upheld this argument and ruled that the dismissal was automatically unfair.

CHAPTER 7

RIGHT TO REQUEST FLEXIBLE WORKING

INTRODUCTION

Under s.80F of the **Employment Rights Act 1996**, employees (both male and female) who have at least 26 weeks' continuous service with their employer have the statutory right to request flexible working, ie the right to apply to their employer for a change to their pattern of working hours and/or the opportunity to work from home. It is important to note that this is a right to request flexible working, and not a right to have it on demand.

When the legislation was originally introduced in April 2003, the right applied only to employees with parental responsibility for a child under six years of age (or age 18, if the child was disabled). In April 2007, the right was made available to employees who had caring responsibilities for a dependent adult, then in April 2009, it was extended to employees with parental responsibility for children up to age 17 (instead of age six).

As from 30 June 2014, the right to request flexible working is available to all employees (irrespective of their caring responsibilities) provided they have at least 26 weeks' continuous service at the time the request is made.

The right to request flexible working is accompanied by a corresponding duty on employers to consider employees' requests in a reasonable manner and not to refuse a valid request unless there is a business reason justifying refusal that falls within a statutory list of business reasons defined in the legislation.

The right to request flexible working is available only to employees, ie those engaged on contracts of employment and not, for example, to casual workers, temporary agency workers, contractors or self-employed people.

ENTITLEMENT TO MAKE A REQUEST

For many employees, the need for flexible working may arise as a consequence of the need to balance the demands of childcare with those of work. Since 30 June 2014, however, the right to request flexible working is available to all employees irrespective of their caring responsibilities, provided they have least 26 weeks' continuous service as at the date the request is made. Employees are not obliged to state their reason for making a request.

Apart from the 26 weeks' continuous service requirement, the only eligibility restriction is that the employee must not have submitted an earlier application for flexible working within the previous 12 months.

MEANING OF "FLEXIBLE WORKING"

"Flexible working" in the context of the relevant legislation does not mean having flexi-time rights or days/hours of work that are entirely flexible. A request for "flexible working" is defined in the legislation as a request for one or more of the following:

- a reduction in the number of hours the employee works (eg a switch from full-time to part-time working)
- a change to the times that the employee works, for example, to the employee's start and/or finish times, shift pattern or days of the week worked
- an arrangement to work wholly or partly from home.

A request for flexible working can, therefore, involve a request for shorter working hours or a shorter working week, a nine-day fortnight, different start and finish times, different days of the week, annualised hours, job sharing, term-time working, exemption from shift working, etc. A request can also include a request to perform all or part of an employee's work from home.

CRITERIA FOR A REQUEST TO BE VALID

In order for an employee's request for flexible working to be valid, it must meet all the following criteria. The request must:

- be in writing
- be dated
- state that it is an application based on the statutory right to request flexible working
- detail the working pattern that the employee wants
- state a proposed date for the new working pattern to come into effect
- outline the effect(s) the employee thinks the pattern of flexible working requested will have on the employer and how, in the employee's opinion, this could be managed
- state whether a previous application for flexible working has been made in the last year and, if so, when it was made.

If an employee submits a request for flexible working that does not include all the above information, the employer is, technically, not under a duty to deal with it. Refusing to deal with such a request would not, however, be good practice and the employer would be better advised to ask the employee to re-submit the request in such a way that it contains the correct information, giving any necessary assistance to the employee to do so. Alternatively, employers are free to deal with requests irrespective of the manner in which they are submitted. Information about (for example) the effect the desired pattern of flexible working might have on the employer and how that could be managed can be discussed at a meeting set up for that purpose.

DEALING WITH A REQUEST

On receipt of a valid request for flexible working, the employer must, by law, deal with it "in a reasonable manner". There is no formal procedure (the previous mandatory procedure for dealing with requests for flexible working was abolished with effect from 30 June 2014). There is, however, a statutory code of practice published by the Advisory, Conciliatory and Arbitration Service (Acas) which sets out the principles that employers should follow when dealing with requests for flexible working (see next section).

It is good practice for the employer to arrange to meet with the employee to discuss the request (and this is recommended by Acas). The meeting can be used to discuss the implications of the proposed new working pattern, for example, if the employee has asked to switch from full-time to part-time working, the employer might wish to make sure that the employee has fully thought through the financial implications for him or her of such a change. Where the employee's proposed pattern of working may, in the employer's view, not be workable, the meeting can be used to explore alternatives. For example, an employee who wishes to reduce the number of hours he or she works may be flexible as regards the days of the week and/or pattern of hours that he or she could work.

Where the employer is prepared immediately to agree to the employee's request, the meeting may be used simply to confirm that fact and agree when the new pattern of working will start.

The employer is under a duty to notify the employee of its decision within a period of three months of the application (unless an extension of time is agreed). This three-month period would include the time required to deal with any appeal the employee might raise against his or her employer's decision to refuse a request.

Confirmation of the new hours of work and/or place of work (and any other consequential contractual changes such as a reduction in pay) must be issued to the employee in writing within four weeks of the new arrangement taking effect.

Acas Code of Practice

Acas has produced a statutory Code of Practice which sets out the principles that employers should follow when dealing with requests for flexible working. The Code is not legally binding but employment tribunals will take its provisions into account when hearing complaints against the employer. It is, therefore, advisable for employers to follow the provisions of the Code which states that, on receipt of a request for flexible working, an employer should:

- arrange to talk to the employee as soon as possible (unless the intention is to approve the request straight away)
- discuss the employee's request directly with him or her, where possible in private
- allow the employee, if he or she wishes, to be accompanied by a colleague at any meeting set up to discuss flexible working
- inform the employee of the decision in writing as soon as possible
- if the employee's request is granted, discuss with him or her when and how the changes might best be implemented
- if the employee's request is rejected, ensure that the rejection is for one of the business reasons permitted by legislation
- allow the employee to appeal the decision.

Acas has also produced a separate non-statutory guide that provides good practice guidance for employers when dealing with requests for flexible working.

Granting a Request

Where an employer agrees to an employee's request for flexible working, the resultant change to the employee's working pattern will amount to a permanent variation to the employee's terms and conditions of employment, unless expressly agreed otherwise. The employer must, within four weeks, write to the employee specifying the contract variations that have been agreed and the date on which they are to take effect.

Although the default position is that a request for flexible working that has been agreed will amount to a permanent variation to the employee's contract, there is nothing to stop the employer and the employee from agreeing at a later date to further changes to the employee's working pattern. Under the legislation, however, once a new pattern of flexible working has been agreed, neither the employer nor the employee has the automatic right to insist on any further changes, nor on reversion to the employee's previous working pattern, if, for example, the employee's circumstances subsequently change.

Temporary Arrangements and Trial Periods

Notwithstanding the provisions described in the previous section, there is no reason why an employer and employee cannot agree on a temporary change to an employee's working hours. In this case the employer should write to the employee stating clearly that the variation to the employee's working pattern is a temporary arrangement, and stating the start and end date of the agreed arrangement.

Equally, although there is no obligation to do so, it is open to the employer and employee to agree a trial period so as to establish whether the proposed new working pattern is suitable for both parties in the longer term. If a trial period is agreed, the employer should clearly record that any variation to the employee's hours or place of work is a temporary measure and state the date on which the trial period will end (at which time a decision would have to be made on whether to agree to permanent changes to the employee's terms of employment). This approach would give the employer an opportunity to ascertain whether the proposed revised pattern of working was actually suitable.

Such a course of action should, however, be undertaken only with the employee's express agreement.

Grounds for Refusing a Request

If the employer decides to refuse an employee's request for flexible working, the employer must inform the employee of this fact and set out the ground on which the refusal is based in writing.

Employers may only refuse an application for flexible working if one or more of the following grounds applies:

- the burden of additional costs
- a detrimental effect on the ability to meet customer demand
- inability to reorganise work among existing staff
- inability to recruit additional staff
- a detrimental impact on quality or performance
- insufficiency of work during the periods the employee proposes to work
- planned structural changes.

These grounds are set out in s.80G of the **Employment Rights Act 1996**. It is not open to an employer to refuse a request on any other grounds, no matter how valid the employer might think another ground for refusal might be. Neither management preference nor perceived inconvenience will amount to a valid ground for refusing a request.

It is worth noting also that agreeing to one employee's request for flexible working does not set a precedent for other employees to demand similar changes to their working hours. Each request stands to be dealt with independently and should be objectively assessed in accordance with the relevant circumstances at the time.

Following the abolition of the statutory procedure for handling requests for flexible working (on 30 June 2014), there is no longer any duty on the employer to permit an employee whose request for flexible working is refused to appeal against that decision. However, it remains good practice to do so. In most cases, the employer's normal grievance procedure could be used to handle appeals.

DISMISSAL AND DETRIMENT

Employees have the right not to be dismissed, selected for redundancy or subjected to any detriment by their employers on the grounds that they applied for flexible working or challenged any alleged infringement of their rights. Detriment could, for example, be a refusal to promote the employee or a denial of training.

If an employee is dismissed as a result of submitting a request for flexible working, the dismissal will be automatically unfair. No qualifying period of service is needed to bring a claim to an employment tribunal in these circumstances and no upper age limit applies.

A complaint to tribunal must normally be made within three months of the date of the matter complained of.

COMPLAINTS AND REMEDIES

An employee whose application for flexible working has been rejected by his or her employer may complain to an employment tribunal (within three months of the date of the matter complained of) in any of the following circumstances, where:

- the employer has failed to respond to the request in a reasonable manner within three months (or at all)
- the employer has wrongly treated the request as withdrawn
- the reason given for refusing the request was false or was not one of the permitted reasons (or where no reason was given), or
- the employee can demonstrate that the decision to reject his or her request was based on incorrect facts.

An employee does not, however, have the right to challenge or question any of the business reasons specified by the employer as the reason for rejecting his or her application. Thus, even if an employee disagrees with the business reason given for refusing the request, this does not constitute grounds for a complaint to the tribunal.

As an alternative to bringing a claim to an employment tribunal, an employee may (with his or her employer's agreement, but not otherwise) refer a "flexible working procedural dispute" to arbitration by an Acas-appointed independent arbitrator under the Acas Arbitration Scheme. The decision of the arbitrator is final and binding.

Should an employment tribunal (or arbitrator) rule that an employee's complaint is well founded, the employer will be ordered to reconsider the employee's application and/or pay the employee compensation in an amount that the tribunal or arbitrator considers to be just and equitable in all the circumstances. Compensation is limited to a maximum of eight weeks' pay, subject to the statutory maximum amount of a week's pay imposed by the Government (which is £475 per week, as from 6 April 2015).

INDEX